AF488183

that isn't always an easy path; it's explanations and honest advice from a successful artist and businesswoman.  For those starting in this field, this book is a guiding hand to working in the industry, presented in such a way that not only instructs, but encourages and mentors at the same time.  Thank you so much, Rhonda, for this book."

**Toni Elliott**—Costume Designer for Film, Theatre, and Opera

"Rhonda brings a rare combination of experience, reliability, and creativity to every production. Hair and make-up are essential to creating the world of a film, and she has an exceptional ability to discuss, prepare, and refine looks in advance, so that by the time you're on set, the process is seamless and fine-tuned. Her insight consistently fosters a successful, creative, and collaborative environment, making her an invaluable member of any film team. I have always deeply appreciated the years of experience, reliability, and creativity that Rhonda brings to the set, and now she shares this in her book *Behind the Scenes as a Makeup Artist for Film*."

**Jenny Alexander**—Senior Producer at Northernlight Productions.

"*Behind the Scenes as a Makeup Artist for Film* is a well written and highly educational book that provides an inside look into the world of professional makeup artistry. Rhonda shares eloquently the technical skills and artistry for film work, and behind the scenes knowledge and resources that are essential for success. The writing is clear, engaging, heartfelt, and approachable, making it valuable for aspiring artists and professionals alike. The book is an excellent teaching tool and a must read for anyone interested in the creative side of makeup for films. Thank you, Rhonda, for sharing and caring!"

**An Hinds**—President Emeritus, Catherine Hinds Institute of Esthetics

"I LOVE your book! You have had an exciting career and it's still going strong! The information you provide is worth a million bucks to anyone considering a career as a MUA or even those already doing the work. The personal experiences you give and how they have helped you along your path illustrate that determination, hard work, a love of work, listening, curiosity, preparation, and simple kindness to fellow humans can help make a person successful."

**Anne Tubiolo**—Film producer, director, and owner of Spotted Bird Productions

"Wow, you have accomplished so much! Your contributions to the field of Makeup Artistry span far beyond education, you've built a legacy that touches many facets

of industry. The *Gift of Mentorship* is a brilliant concept and such a powerful way to begin the book. Your section on *Endorsements* truly resonated with me; it's one of my favorite parts and so true that enthusiasm and support really are contagious. I genuinely can't think of anyone more perfect to bring this message to life in a book."
**Jaclyn Luongo**—Aesthetician, makeup artist, and author

"There is no better advice than that coming from an expert that has been "in the trenches" and has seen it all. Rhonda does an excellent job incorporating her years of experience into content that is beyond relatable to seasoned professionals as well as new artists. Her book is sure to provide a solid foundation for what to expect, how to pivot and how to succeed as a makeup artist in the film industry. Job well done!"
**Michelle D'Allaird-Brenner**—Owner of Aesthetic Science Institute in New York, a CIDESCO Diplomat, and author

"*Behind the Scenes as a Makeup Artist for Film* is as entertaining as it is informative. Rhonda's ability to tell this story is exceptional. She instantly draws you in, and welcomes you like a friend sitting down for a conversation over coffee. Rhonda's humble and lovable nature alongside her extensive knowledge within the beauty industry makes this memoir invaluable. A must-read for every aspiring film and theater makeup and hair artist."
**Rozy Dahlstedt**—Hair/Makeup Artist for film and songwriter-singer for *Anktana*

"Well done! A wealth of knowledge and very easy to understand. Great attention to detail of every procedure presented. I learned a great deal not only about film makeup but also a side of you that I never had the privilege of knowing personally as well as professionally. A sure industry "best seller". Congratulations!"
**Terry Kenney**—BSHS; holistic aesthetician, skin salon owner, instructor, and author

"Reading *Behind the Scenes as a Makeup Artist for Film*, I was struck by the depth of experience and artistry my friend infused into every page. It's clear how much care went into collecting the stories, techniques, and wisdom that shaped her journey—from inspiring mentors to talented collaborators in the film industry. As I read, I could vividly imagine her crafting wounds and scars, conceal imperfections, and transform actors for their roles, all while teaching her craft with grace and generosity."
**Shirley Sarpi**—Cosmetologist and beauty consultant.

*"Behind the Scenes as a Makeup Artist for Film* is a book for the seasoned professional, the novice, and for a person simply wanting to read about the world of make-up and the world of filmmaking. She goes into details about all aspects of make-up and delves into various experiences on sets. You learn all about who works on these film sets, their jobs and their relationships with the film industry. You learn about how make-up artistry affects the film, techniques, and the structure of the days. It's a book for those already in the industry and for those wanting a peek into the world of filmmaking, a window and a mirror. Excellent must read."

**Andrea Lyman**—Actor and New England Local President of SAGAFTRA

# BEHIND THE SCENES AS A
# MAKEUP ARTIST FOR FILM

# BEHIND THE SCENES AS A MAKEUP ARTIST FOR FILM

## Set Life Realities and Lessons From One Artist's Journey

Rhonda Cummings

Published by Rc Makeup Artist

ISBN (hardcover): 979-8-9986393-0-2
ISBN (ebook): 978-8-9986393-1-9

Book design and production by www.AuthorSuccess.com


Printed in the United States of America

# Dedication

To my Mom,

My greatest mentor, cheerleader, encourager, and friend. So many of these pages were written while sitting at your kitchen table, your presence beside me more comforting than I could ever put into words. I still hear your teacup gently settling onto the table as you took a sip and listened patiently while I read my latest paragraphs out loud. You always smiled with me, always encouraged me, and always believed in me, especially when I struggled to believe in myself.

When you could no longer sit with me at the table, I made sure to keep you updated on the latest chapter, because sharing this journey with you mattered just as much as finishing the book itself. Thank you, Mom. I feel you watching over me, my angel at the finish line, and this is as much yours as it is mine!

xxoo

# CONTENTS

# Author's Note

This book, *Behind the Scenes as a Makeup Artist for Film*, is a collection of my personal experiences throughout my career as a makeup artist. Every story shared reflects moments I've lived, lessons I've learned, and the creative challenges I've faced behind the scenes. This is my story.

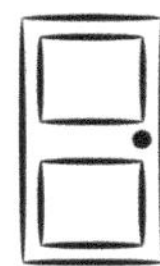



# Step Inside the Real World of Film Makeup

What does it really take to become a successful makeup artist in the film industry? That's the question I asked myself often throughout my journey, and it's the question that inspired me to write this book to share with others.

*Behind the Scenes as a Makeup Artist for Film* is more than a memoir of my path—it's an honest, unfiltered guide from forty years of experience in beauty, education, and film. I began my career at eighteen, but it wasn't until I turned fifty-two that my dream of working in film truly took flight. Now, at sixty-seven, I've had the honor of serving as director of hair and makeup on more than a dozen independent films and commercials for television, and I have trained over 1,000 beauty professionals in the art of makeup.

This book is for those who are ready to take makeup artistry into the real world of film. I'll share with you how I dealt with pre-production, life on set, post-wrap expectations, and much more. I wish someone had shared this information with me when I was just starting out.

If you're serious about becoming a makeup artist for film, I hope these pages will guide, inspire, and empower you as you pursue your own journey.

# Welcome, Future Film Makeup Artist!

*Behind the Scenes as a Makeup Artist for Film* is a collection of my personal stories, lessons, and real-world insights gathered over nearly four decades in the industry. As the department head of hair and makeup for more than a dozen independent films and countless commercial projects, I've faced challenges that were as unpredictable as they were rewarding.

This book is designed to show you what it is truly like to work as a professional makeup artist on a film set and what it takes to get there. You will discover why the role of makeup director is more than simply brushes and colorful palettes; it is about collaborating with producers, directors, costume designers, and actors. The work begins before the first pre-production meeting and continues through the filming of the final scene. You will also learn that your role may include managing the budget, sourcing supplies, and, when necessary, hiring an additional makeup artist.

In these pages, I'll guide you on how to build a strong and versatile portfolio and professional makeup kits. You'll gain insight into why networking is essential for landing future jobs in the film industry. I'll also show you how to work effectively with film crew members and explain why they play a crucial role in your success. Finally, I'll walk you through five specific steps you can take right now to jumpstart your film makeup career.

Whether you're just starting out or dreaming of one day leading your own makeup department, my hope is that this book gives you the confidence, clarity, and inspiration to move forward.

REV WAR
ROLL
SCENE
TAKE
A 01
S9 DIANA
1
Director
JILL
Camera
STEVE SHERRICK
Date 8-15-23
MOS DAY NITE

# CHAPTER 1
# Road Map of Inspiration

When a film's executive producer contacts me and invites me to join their film crew, my enthusiasm is immediately sparked! It's game on! Being involved right from the beginning is a tremendous privilege. A special highlight for me is when I've collaborated with them prior, and they request to work with me again. It signifies that they value my past contributions. Achieving this level of synergy requires hard work. I've collaborated with numerous production companies that appreciate me for my thoroughness and ability to adapt to last-minute changes.

## Collaboration is Key

I've learned that collaboration isn't just helpful, it's essential. If you want to be successful in this specialized field of makeup, you must understand that working closely with others is part of your job. Open communication with the executive producer, executive director, and the gaffer is crucial, but it doesn't stop there. You also need to build strong connections with the costume designer and the actors.

Why? Because we're all working toward the same goal: bringing every character to life in a believable, compelling way, as the manuscript has guided us. Your makeup design must align with the wardrobe, the lighting, the storyline, and the actor's performance. That level of unity only happens when everyone is on the same page, and that means being open, communicative, and willing to listen.

When you collaborate well, your work will stand out. You'll avoid costly mistakes, solve problems faster, and earn the trust of fellow film crew members. More importantly, you'll grow creatively. The best ideas often emerge from shared insights, rather than working in isolation. So, if you care about your craft and want to thrive in this industry, make collaboration a priority. It's not optional; it's one of the most indispensable traits you can have.

## My Journey

The commencement of my journey unfolded the day after I graduated from Peabody Veterans Memorial High School in 1976. It was a Monday morning, and my Mom let me use her 1972 burgundy station wagon to drive to Fazio's Institute of Beauty Culture in Lawrence, Massachusetts. My goal was to enroll in school full-time for nine months, which spanned 1,000 hours. I chose this school as it stood out as one of the leaders in this trade, and it was offering continuing education to all its licensed cosmetology graduates. A letter soon arrived confirming my acceptance into Fazio's on May 24, 1976.

I vividly recall the first day of "beauty school" as if it happened just yesterday. That moment marked the commencement of my career! As I crossed the threshold of the grand brick two-story building nestled on the main street in the town, my heart brimmed with excitement as I ascended fifty steps up to the second floor. Each step presented itself as a physical challenge, but with resolute determination, I reminded myself that completing beauty schooling was the initial step toward a promising career. My plans involved initiating a two-year apprenticeship promptly after graduation to meet the criteria for the Massachusetts state boards. The next three years were clearly spoken for, but I welcomed the commitment wholeheartedly.

On the very first day of beauty school, I presented myself in a freshly acquired, pristine white uniform, matching white shoes and socks, with sleekly pulled-back hair and impeccably manicured fingernails, and carrying the beauty kit provided upon my commitment to the role as a beauty school attendee.

As I reached the top of the staircase, I paused to take a deep breath before stepping into this new world. I whispered to myself, "Here we go," then I opened the door. The distinct scents of hairspray and permanent wave solution enveloped me immediately. With a huge smile on my face, I took my first few steps into the front reception area and said out loud, "I'm finally home!"

I easily adapted to the routine of attending Fazio's five days a week from 9:00 a.m. to 4:30 p.m. Every morning for nine months, at 7:30 a.m., I embarked on a forty-five-minute journey in my recently acquired 1975 red Ford Granada, a secondhand treasure generously gifted by my parents. I held a profound affection for that car, treating it as if it were truly my own. While my Dad covered the initial car expenses and assisted with fuel costs, our agreement stipulated that the vehicle was exclusively mine for all school-related responsibilities and work, contingent upon my maintaining exemplary grades and making timely payments on the balance of school tuition. I was confident in my ability to uphold my end of the bargain, having diligently worked and saved nearly every penny throughout the preceding year. This prudent approach allowed me to contribute more than half of the tuition upfront, ensuring that the subsequent monthly payments were manageable for me. I also continued to work part-time on Friday and Saturday evenings from 5:00 p.m. to 11:30 p.m. and all day every Sunday as a hostess at Augustine's Italian Restaurant.

# The Gift of Mentorships

Reflecting on the early days, I recall the challenges of obtaining resources before the convenience of YouTube and the internet. My options were very limited. I had to purchase used books from local bookstores or make a trip to the library to find valuable information. Over the years, I've accumulated a collection of more than two hundred books to enhance my knowledge. Many of them were first acquired at second-hand bookstores and then eventually online. When mentoring a new makeup artist, one of my favorite gestures is to give them a book from my collection.

Invaluable mentorships will provide you with guidance, support, significant value, and wisdom. The mentor's wealth of experience and expertise allows them to offer valuable insights tailored to your specific needs and challenges. They empower you to develop skills and confidence, while providing constructive feedback for improvement. Additionally, the mentor facilitates connections with valuable networks and opportunities.

As I encountered various mentors, they evolved into trusted advisers, offering education and assistance in building connections that provided me with a competitive advantage. Many of them played a pivotal role in shaping the professional I am today, and I cherish each one dearly. This profound gratitude fueled my passion to give back as a mentor myself.

## MRS. JAY

It wasn't long before I understood the significance of having a mentor. I discovered immense joy during my beauty school time, especially in the classes led by Mrs. Jay, who was the seasoned instructor and later took on the role of my mentor. She fulfilled this role exceptionally well, and it proved invaluable to me. She was the perfect description of what a mentor is: a special person eager to share her experiences, guide me, and facilitate my learning through observation.

Mrs. Jay was an icon, having actively participated in both the Massachusetts Hair Design Team and the USA National Hair Team for many years. Standing at a petite four feet ten inches, she exuded elegance. When she wore high-heeled stiletto shoes, we could see eye to eye. Her signature bleached-blonde hair was consistently styled into a stunning updo, and her smile spread from ear to ear.

Around the fourth month of our schooling, after completing our theoretical coursework and assessments, I dove into my first hair coloring class led by Mrs. Jay. The class was rigorous, and a week later, I had the privilege of applying hair color to her hair, a task I repeated a few more times thereafter. I relished the experience as it provided an opportunity for me to gain insights and knowledge.

Mrs. Jay developed a fondness for both me and my new cosmetology friend, Caren. Caren and I began and completed our cosmetology school journey simultaneously. Our instant connection led to a strong friendship, and we became partners in various school activities. Our adventures at beauty school were particularly memorable, and soon enough, we found ourselves in the position of being the teacher's pets. During lunch breaks, we would routinely check the teacher's office to see if anyone needed coffee or lunch. One day, Mrs. Jay approached us with an exciting proposition, asking if we would be willing to serve as hair models for an advanced hair-cutting class she was conducting in a few days for licensed hairdressers at our school. Without hesitation, we both enthusiastically agreed to be hair models.

Fazio's was renowned for hosting advanced classes for licensed cosmetologists on a monthly basis, and at the helm was Mrs. Jay. It was in this dynamic environment that Caren and I had the privilege of seeing first-hand the latest haircuts, hair coloring techniques, salon jargon, and business insights. These experiences served as invaluable tools as we pursued our aspirations of becoming successful salon owners. Even when we weren't modeling for her, we actively contributed as her first-hand assistants, assisting in preparing models by washing their hair and touching up their makeup.

I am grateful to Mrs. Jay for the wealth of knowledge she imparted and for leaving an indelible mark on my understanding of how to uphold the highest standards as a cosmetology instructor. She also encouraged me to volunteer and be part of the Massachusetts Cosmetology Support Group and try out for the Massachusetts Design Team, which I successfully joined in the mid-1980s and remained a part of until the early 1990s.

One of the most exhilarating moments in my career occurred when she reached out to me years later, seeking advice on pre- and post-skincare because she was considering having facial cosmetic surgery. The memory of that call still brings a smile to my face. Once again, thank you, Mrs. Jay, for being one of my most significant mentors and a major influence on shaping my professional journey.

### ROSIE

I consider myself incredibly fortunate to have had another significant figure in my life. In 1978, Rosie, a close friend of my mother's and her personal hairdresser, offered me my first apprenticeship job after I graduated from beauty school. I can still recall the days of my elementary school years when I eagerly accompanied my Mom to the salon many Saturday mornings at 8:00 a.m., where I had the privilege of witnessing her work magic on my Mom's hair.

One certainty in life was my Mom's unwavering commitment to her Saturday morning appointments for her weekly hair session. The only reason she would miss a hair appointment was if she felt ill or faced the rare obstacle of a New England snowstorm, as she would not drive in the snow. Regardless of financial constraints, my Mom prioritized her weekly hairdresser visit right into the house budget. Smart move!

When I got to go with her on a Saturday morning, I felt important walking into the salon. The smell of hairspray and permanent wave solution would wake up my nostrils and water my eyes for a few seconds every time. But I loved it! Everyone said hi to me and Mom as we hung up our coats and were escorted to the washing stations in the back of this modern-day salon. As I followed, I would observe all the funky hair stations and the beauticians (that's what they were called back then) working on clients. There were eight separate hair stations, all decorated to the liking of each professional. All of the beauticians were busy servicing and engaging in conversations with their clients.

Eventually, Mom settled into Rosie's chair after having her head shampooed and massaged. I always sat across the room in a hair-drying chair that had a huge hood attached to it, used to dry rollers in your hair. I remember I would sit there for about an hour, mesmerized as my eyes wandered to the left and then to the right. Back and forth, my head would bounce as I observed the inside operations of a salon. I loved it!

As I grew older, my responsibility as the babysitter for my five siblings prevented me from accompanying my Mom on Saturday mornings. Yet, I gladly took on the role, knowing my Mom deserved time for herself while raising six kids.

Several years down the road, as I embarked on my senior year in high school, Rosie acquired a local salon where she had been working. With genuine encouragement, she suggested that I pursue cosmetology school. She conveyed that upon completing the program and obtaining my 1,000-hour diploma, I should pay her a visit. True to her advice, a year later, I proudly fulfilled that promise.

# Building Momentum

The day after I took my state board exam, I received a call from the licensing board that I had passed! I immediately drove my 1976 red Ford Granada to Rosie's house, as the salon was closed on Mondays and Tuesdays. Despite her absence from her home, I patiently waited for her return for two hours as I sat on the top step of her front stairs. I tightly held my 1,000-hour diploma in my left hand while intermittently taking drags from a cigarette in my right. All I could envision was becoming her assistant for the next two years, fulfilling the apprenticeship requirement before taking the state exam, and perhaps eventually owning her salon upon her retirement.

When Rosie finally pulled into her driveway, she immediately spotted me on the stairs, wearing the biggest smile. Without words, she sensed that I had successfully passed my cosmetology state board exam and was holding my permit to work. Rushing over, we embraced, and in that moment, my dream had become a reality. She promptly offered me a full-time position at the salon, and three years later, I assumed ownership while she opted to stay on as an independent subcontractor with us for a year. I am immensely grateful for her decision, as during that time, she taught me invaluable lessons about the business aspects of running a salon. Thank you, Rosie! Our business and friendship relationship will forever be cherished.

## NEW SALON OWNER

The salon was nestled inside a hotel that had been constructed in the mid-1970s. It was the biggest hotel north of Boston at that time, and the grand ballroom inside added to the allure. In the 1980s, a few cities north of Boston boasted theaters and large entertainment venues, and this positioned the hotel at the heart of this lively scene.

Situated to the right of the front desk, the salon was visible to every guest who checked into the hotel. During my early days working as an apprentice for Rosie, I often catered to walk-ins, primarily hotel patrons seeking hair services. Despite the salon's local client base being consistently booked, I had the opportunity to attend to walk-in clients. I was Rosie's assistant, and occasionally, one of the walk-ins would be a celebrity who would grace our salon, especially those performing at nearby theaters and entertainment venues.

Taking on the role of being a new salon owner was a blend of excitement and fear. More accurately, it was downright hectic. Balancing life included my marriage, raising our three-year-old twin boys, and managing a full staff at the salon five days a week, which added a layer of complexity. I could never have done this without the help of my husband, Allen.

The salon's popularity soared with an increase in younger clients and with appointments scheduled for four to five weeks in advance. The salon's location within the hotel continued to prove financially sound. Meanwhile, my husband Allen, juggling a full-time job at General Electric, played the role of cook, bottle washer, and housekeeper whenever I was at work. My husband worked a rotating schedule, so when he worked the first shift, I would work the second shift at the salon and vice versa. We always made it work, especially with the help of family.

Amidst the daily chaos at the salon, some of my fondest memories revolved around the chance to host educational events for local beauty suppliers. These events were special occasions where these companies utilized my salon to feature renowned educators. The grand ballroom at the hotel and my salon served as the perfect venue. The convenience of using my salon spared these companies the need to rely on typical ladies' rooms for washing their models' heads. In return for the privilege, they generously supplied me with a retail inventory of their product. It was truly a win-win situation.

Every month, I had the privilege of witnessing renowned cosmetologists and makeup artists (MUAs) transform stage models right before my eyes in my salon. This is how I initially grasped the concept of "perception in distance" when it comes to applying stage makeup. The idea is to ensure that both the person in the first row and the one at the back of the room can clearly see the model's face from the stage. It's a remarkable skill, and I had the front-row seat once again to marvel at their craftsmanship. The experience became even more exhilarating when they would occasionally invite me to assist them. My passion for stage makeup applications flourished during these moments. Subsequently, I began developing significant connections in the beauty industry, ultimately leading me to the position I hold today.

Before long, the salon team was not only booked throughout the week but also for gigs every weekend. Whether it was a wedding, a photoshoot, or a commercial assignment, we worked tirelessly and earned a good income.

I continued managing the salon until the late 1980s, as the demands of overseeing salon staff and engaging in freelancing, which I loved, became overwhelming. I finally made the decision to sell the business to Bobby Thomson, who was working at the salon. I consider myself fortunate to have had Bobby as part of the salon team, as he stands out as one of the finest professionals I've ever had the pleasure of working with. Thank you, Bobby!

## FACE FORWARD INC.

After selling the salon, I felt a spark I couldn't ignore—a pull toward a new chapter. That's when I launched my own subcontracting hair and makeup business, *Face Forward Inc.* Starting fresh was both exhilarating and a little terrifying, but it turned out to be one of the most rewarding decisions I ever made. It gave me the freedom to work fewer hours, earn more, and shape my career on my own terms.

Many artists at the time were heading to New York to join the Makeup Union, but in 1984, disappearing for weeks on a film set wasn't an option for me—I had a young family and responsibilities at home. With my children a bit older and my husband, Allen, cheering me on, I carved out my own path as an independent MUA, taking on commercial and film subcontracting work. It was the perfect blend of creativity, flexibility, and adventure.

I owe so much to the salon reps who supported me during my nine years at The Den Unisex Salon. They believed in me before I fully believed in myself, and the opportunities they offered shaped the artist I became. I hold those early memories with deep gratitude.

One of my very first assignments as a makeup artist was with the extraordinary Shirley Sarpi of Sarpi Salon in Saugus, Massachusetts. Shirley was—and still is—one of the top educators for a major professional hair color brand, and every time I worked with her, I felt like stepping into a master class.

When Shirley took the stage beside her gleaming silver hydraulic chair, she commanded the room like a queen in her element. Hundreds of cosmetologists hung onto her every word, and backstage, my team and I were buzzing with energy, preparing models for their grand reveal. Her passion was contagious. Whenever I think of those shows, I still smile. Shirley and I even teamed up for a fundraising event at a Boston nightclub with local sports celebrities—one of many unforgettable moments. Thank you, Shirley. We truly had a blast.

Around the same time, I met someone who would become a lifelong friend: Tina McCaffrey. We first crossed paths at a beauty pageant in western Massachusetts, both working as HMU artists for the contestants. Little did we know that meeting would spark a friendship that has lasted thirty-six years—filled with travel, laughter, and more adventures than I could ever fit into a single chapter. Tina has always been my right-hand woman and a true gift in my life.

At that same pageant, I also met the talented Madonna Harris, a highly skilled MUA with an impressive résumé. Recognizing both women's talent, I invited Tina and Madonna to join me as trainers at

Face Forward, and they said yes without hesitation. When the Massachusetts Board of Cosmetology approved our Advanced Institute for Cosmetologists, Makeup Artists, and Aestheticians in 2010, we officially became a team. For ten years, the three of us trained aspiring artists together, sharing knowledge, passion, and plenty of laughs along the way.

During the 1980s and 1990s, Boston was the beauty industry's East Coast hotspot, hosting one of the largest and most exciting cosmetology trade shows of the year. Every season, my colleagues and I could hardly wait. Walking onto that convention floor felt like stepping into a living tapestry of innovation—color, texture, technique, and creativity everywhere you turned.

In 1990, while subcontracting as an MUA for a well-known hair color company at the Boston show, I had a chance reunion with Catherine Hinds, the legendary founder of the Catherine Hinds Institute of Aesthetics. I had purchased aesthetic supplies from her manufacturing company in Woburn for years, but this time, she had seen my stage makeup work. She asked whether I held a teaching license (I did!), and right then and there, she offered me a position overseeing the MUA Department at her school.

Those two years working with her and teaching were extraordinary. I helped expand the makeup curriculum and built an advanced course I was incredibly proud of. I also met two remarkable instructors—Terry Kenney and Bernie Rahall—who became mentors, friends, and guiding lights in my aesthetics journey. Thank you both for everything.

I continued teaching and subcontracting HMU projects until late 1993, when a new opportunity changed my direction once again: becoming an exclusive distributor for a national skincare company across all of New England. From 1993 to 2016, skincare became the heart of my work.

I couldn't have done it without my incredible sisters—Denise Mahoney and Julie Sinatra—who were the backbone of the business for twenty-one years. In our early days, my sister, Christine also jumped in to help, and my dear childhood friend, Paula Currier, a plastic surgery nurse-turned-aesthetician, joined us too. She and I worked side by side at countless events and trade shows focused on skin and makeup. We truly did have fun.

As the business grew, so did our team: Michelle DiOrio, Karen de Steuben, Jessica Mogauro, and of course, the unforgettable Tina McCaffrey. We also had amazing part-time help from Kristin and Brittany Cummings, my supportive husband Allen, and my sweet mother, who always showed up with homemade treats for our classes.

Shifting from cosmetology to aesthetics turned the skincare trade show circuit into my world for twenty-one years. Filming stepped aside during that chapter, but I have no regrets. It was exciting, intense, and full of stories I'm still writing about today—stories that will be part of my next memoir.

## Endorsements are Contagious

If you are already a licensed cosmetologist, aesthetician, or certified MUA, now it's time to take bold steps to elevate your career. Keep reaching out. Don't shy away from exploring unconventional opportunities that might lead you somewhere unexpected. When you complete a project, always ask for an endorsement or recommendation. It's not just a pat on the back; it will build credibility on your resume for future gigs. And here's a tip: take a picture with each person who endorses you. That simple snapshot adds visual proof of your professional connections and achievements. Plus, it's fun to share the photo with them as a keepsake. These small but intentional actions build your reputation and network over time. The more consistently you advocate for yourself and document your work, the more doors you'll open. Keep showing up, keep asking questions, and keep growing. Your future in this industry depends on it.

In the early part of my career, I became known for getting hundreds of behind-the-scenes action photographs. Sharing these pics and reminiscing with the film crew made it easy for me to ask for an endorsement or recommendation. I was always honored when they would say, "Of course, I will endorse you and write a letter."

With each film you work on, your confidence will grow, your network will increase, and each project will build a lasting memory for you. It's been forty years since I started my HMU career, and it still is truly a labor of love. The only difference now is that I get to pick and choose the jobs I want to work on. Presently, I'm involved with Tufts University in their annual film project, *Half the History*, which is based on real historical figures. Professor Jennifer Burton is at the helm of this project, alongside her students and Five Sisters Productions. Jennifer is a professor, writer, director, producer, and much more when on a film set. Thank you, Jenn, for fourteen years of memories.

I have also been specializing in HMU for historical documentaries, depicting real historical figures for museum exhibits. A particular joy and specialty of mine lies in the application of facial hair for period films. Crafting and applying mustaches, sideburns, and beards has always been a fascination of mine.

# 1 FINAL KEY THOUGHTS

- ☐ Begin your journey as a MUA in film with the right mindset.
- ☐ Build relationships that lead to future endorsements and referrals.
- ☐ Respect and collaboration are essential; you'll often work repeatedly with the same people.
- ☐ Seek out mentors who are working in your desired film genre.
- ☐ Stay committed, continuously learn, and evolve with each project.
- ☐ Let your passion and persistence guide you for a long, fulfilling career in film.

PROD. Stella
ROLL
A001
SCENE
TAKE
1
DIRECTOR: Jonathan Heutmaker

# CHAPTER 2

# Educational Pathways for Future Film Makeup Artists

When I made the decision to pursue a career in the beauty industry, I quickly realized how critical it was to choose the right educational pathway. I asked myself, *What niche will truly fit me, and what educational route will get me there?*

You will quickly learn that having a clear career goal from the start is essential. Choosing the educational foundation doesn't just shape how prepared you'll be; it also directly impacts how marketable you are in the competitive world of film. The better you're trained and the more specialized your skills, the more value you bring to the table, and that will show in your paycheck.

## "Lights, Camera . . . Education?"

I highly recommend that you research state-licensed accredited schools, whether it's a cosmetology school, an aesthetic institute, or a specialized makeup academy. Learn the core skills you need to get recognized. No matter what pathway you choose, one thing is for certain: you will need proof of professional training when it comes to seeking work in films. Producers and HMU department heads want to know that you've invested in your craft and that you have the credentials to back it up! While unaccredited courses are not inherently without value, attending an accredited school in the beginning is what you need to set yourself apart as a skilled MUA for film.

## COSMETOLOGY SCHOOL

Cosmetology school played a crucial role in laying a solid foundation for my skills in hairstyling and makeup. The school I attended also taught a curriculum on caring for, cutting, and styling wigs. Although I was not aware of its significance at the time, I am now forever grateful for choosing this career.

At a licensed school, you'll also receive a foundational understanding of makeup, provided the school has a well-structured program and an instructor experienced in practical makeup applications. If cosmetology is your chosen path, select a school with a strong reputation for theory in hair dressing, the basics of wig care, and ask about the makeup curriculum.

Your state's cosmetology board is responsible for the approval of schools and the rules and regulations they must adhere to. For example, in Massachusetts, the state mandates a 1,000-hour curriculum that includes everything from hairdressing, skin care, and nail care. Makeup is included in the forty-five hours allocated for skin care, but it is not listed separately with designated hours.

After reviewing this information on their website, I decided to reach out to various cosmetology schools in Massachusetts and ask each how many hours were dedicated to makeup in their curriculum. The response I received from all of them was basically, "We don't have a specific makeup program, but makeup is covered during the skin care portion of our program."

I then asked how many of the forty-five hours of skin care are dedicated to makeup. Unfortunately, none of the schools could provide an exact answer. This lack of clarity about dedicated makeup hours suggests that if hairdressing isn't part of your future, you might want to explore alternatives and avoid wasting a year of your life.

Recalling my own experience in cosmetology school, I remember receiving five days dedicated exclusively to makeup training. It was such a small fraction of the entire program, and once we had our theory classes finished, we graduated from the classroom onto the salon floor, where we could practice hair, nails, and makeup on clients who were getting their hair serviced at the student clinic.

It's always a good idea to check student reviews and inquire about the instructor's background. Ask the school what the teacher-to-student ratio is, both in the classroom and during practical sessions. It's crucial to understand whether a workshop kit is included in your tuition and what it includes. Additionally, find out if the school provides hands-on training, as this is a significant aspect of practical skill development. Being well-informed about these details will help you make an informed decision about which type of schooling best aligns with your goals and expectations.

Don't forget to investigate your local adult vocational trade schools, which usually have evening classes in different trades such as cosmetology and aesthetics. Tuition is usually less expensive than at private schools. I used to love guest-speaking at adult cosmetology programs held at our local trade school.

## AESTHETIC SCHOOL

I know first-hand that the students who graduated from the Catherine Hinds Institute of Aesthetics in the early 1990s received a solid, basic education in the art of makeup, because I taught there at that time. In the 300-hour basic aesthetic program at C.E. Hinds, Catherine asked me to revise the makeup curriculum to include a total of twenty-one hours in class, plus I assigned homework. For those continuing with the 600-hour advanced skincare program, I created an advanced class that included camouflage therapy makeup, giving the students an additional twenty-one hours for a total of forty-two hours of makeup instruction within their 600 hours.

I continued teaching at the C.E.H Institute for the next two years before deciding to hit the road and specialize as a freelance makeup artist.

### MAKEUP SCHOOL

With so many private makeup schools across the United States, you need to narrow down your options to those specifically offering accredited training for the film industry. Don't settle for any program; look for one with a detailed curriculum that thrives on theory, techniques, color theory, special effects, designing with crepe hair, and so much more for various genres. You'll need a comprehensive course to better prepare you for the demands of the film industry and to help you understand the *why* behind every brushstroke and product choice.

If your passion lies in special effects makeup (SFX-MU), then focus your search on schools that offer hands-on training in that area. Whether you're dreaming of creating realistic injuries, transforming faces with prosthetics, or mastering aging makeup, the proper education can shape your future. Don't be afraid to ask questions, request a tour, or even speak to alumni of the school. This is your career, and your creative journey, so make sure you start with the training that sets you up for success in the world of film.

After completing your formal schooling, I recommend that you explore opportunities for continuing education. Search for courses that prioritize theory as well as practical application. Securing a position in the field or participating in an apprenticeship can be beneficial to you. Consider reaching out to nearby colleges with theater and film programs, as they often collaborate with MUAs to instruct students on character makeup for self-application in their theatrical productions.

## Fueling Your Curiosity

I enjoy reading about renowned MUAs who have made it big. This passion has persisted throughout my career and continues to fuel my curiosity. Early on, I discovered that studying their journey, particularly before they attained fame, offers invaluable insights into the intricacies of how they became a MUA for film. I loved exploring their contributions across so many different film genres, observing their credits and accolades. This approach has significantly enriched my understanding of various genres. I also enjoy researching accomplished MUAs who have left an indelible mark on the film industry.

Each year, I'm on the lookout for the yearly motion picture awards on television, especially the ones that recognize HMU's and MUAs from various genres. The most common are romance, drama, action, mystery, western, animation, science fiction, adventure, comedy, and musical, just to name the most popular. Many film productions combine two or more genres in one film. For some interesting reading, go online and type in Academy Awards for best makeup and hairstyling. All the big names are listed with their film credits. I enjoy reading it yearly to see who the new MUAs are and check on my favorites. Winning an award is exciting, but it's all about the artist!

One of my top favorite awards is given by the Hollywood Makeup Artist and Hair Stylist Guild Awards (MUAHS). It recognizes "Outstanding Achievements in Makeup and Hair" across television, film, and commercials. Below are some other noteworthy awards for outstanding work in cinema.

## THE SATURN AWARD

"Best Makeup of the Year for a Genre Film," first presented in 1974 by the Academy of Science Fiction, Fantasy, and Horror Films for Outstanding Makeup Special Effects.

## THE OSCARS AWARD

The Academy of Motion Picture Arts and Sciences (better known as the Oscars) was first created in 1927, but not until 1981 did it have a category for "Best Makeup in Film" to recognize excellence in hair and makeup for a motion picture.

## THE GOLDEN GLOBE AWARD

"Best Makeup of the Year for both American and Foreign Outstanding Makeup Artist in a Film."

## THE EMMY AWARDS

"Outstanding Makeup" is presented by the Academy of Television Arts and Sciences for exceptional makeup work for television, TV movies, and TV mini-series.

# Unexpected Pathways

### EXPRESSIONS IN DANCE

Before my initial phase of a beauty career, never mind a makeup career, I became involved with a prominent local dance company called "Expressions in Dance" for four decades under the ownership of Christine King in Peabody, Massachusetts. Christine served as the director and senior educator of this thriving dance school, and I thoroughly enjoyed assisting with makeup during recitals and being backstage amidst all the excitement. This experience became a valuable learning opportunity for me in the realm of stage makeup.

To my surprise, I gained insights into how lighting significantly influenced the final appearance that Christine aimed to convey. This hands-on experience proved to be priceless. At the age of seventeen, this marked my inaugural exposure to the interplay of lighting, stage makeup, and a live stage production. It wasn't until many years later that I realized how valuable being involved behind the scenes of a dance recital was going to be to my future journey.

My connection with Christine spans forty-nine years, and she is truly an exceptional person and dear friend. Fortunately, my youngest son, Michael, and Christine's daughter, Brittney, tied the knot and brought three beautiful grandchildren into all our lives: Ciara, Caylee, and Camron.

## THEATER

In the realm of theater, actors are often responsible for applying their own makeup for each performance. I've taught many students and actors how to apply their makeup to their stage character. Unfortunately, after one makeup lesson with me, my job is completed. Each actor becomes responsible for applying their own stage makeup for every performance. I learned this and so much more when I first met Linda Girard from Tufts University.

It all began more than sixteen years ago when I first had the privilege of collaborating with Linda, a brilliant costume designer and wardrobe instructor at Tufts University. Linda wasn't just an expert in her craft; she was also a warm and thoughtful person who made every encounter a pleasure. I always looked forward to seeing her, especially when she attended advanced makeup courses I taught at my school or when she picked up a purchase order of stage makeup for the theater departments where she instructed the course.

I admired the way she approached her work with such passion and precision. I loved seeing her wardrobe drawings for the next show hanging on the walls of the wardrobe lab. Her work amazed me as I got to see the drawings first-hand, including lots of side notes.

My initial invitation to visit the Tufts University Theater Department came on a Friday afternoon in the fall of 2008. Linda stopped by my work to pick up a makeup order for her theater students. As we chatted about her upcoming semester, she shared her excitement about a production they were preparing for in two months. Then, she extended an invitation that made my heart skip a beat. She asked if I'd come to Tufts to help with makeup and hair for a dress rehearsal and speak to her students about stage makeup techniques. The offer was irresistible. "Absolutely!" I said without hesitation.

Though the stage world had never been my calling, the idea of stepping behind the dynamic, creative world of theater as an MUA was thrilling to me. The chance to share my knowledge with eager students and to see a production come together was an opportunity I couldn't pass up. The thought of standing in the wings, surrounded by costumes, wigs, and that intoxicating blend of anticipation and artistry filled me with energy. I knew this would be a chance to combine my passion for makeup with the electric world of live performance. I couldn't wait to immerse myself in the process and witness the transformation that happens backstage.

The day finally came when I took my first steps into the Tufts University auditorium. Suddenly, a rush of excitement and curiosity swept over me as I pushed open the doors. I could hear the faint murmur of voices and footsteps echoing through the vast space, and the air seemed to be charged with students expelling their creative energy. The stage stood majestic and commanding, its towering curtains gently swaying, as if breathing in anticipation. Even in its emptiness, the space had a sense of magic waiting to be revealed.

Linda came from behind the stage curtain and waved me to come up and follow her. She welcomed me with her warm smile as she guided me backstage and gave me a brief tour before the rehearsal began. The backstage area was a maze of costumes, wigs, and props, each telling its own story. I couldn't help but marvel at the intricacy of it all.

Before rehearsal, I took time to meet with her students and guide them on applying their stage makeup. In addition to working with students, I had the opportunity to prepare hired stage actors involved in the stage production. On this project, my responsibilities expanded to include not only styling the hair and wigs, but also applying and removing the facial hair and makeup the men would be wearing. For this job, I was known as a wig specialist and an SFX MUA for theater.

The entire experience was a beautiful blend of teaching and artistry that deepened my appreciation for the intricate world of theater. Being involved as part of a stage crew allowed me to witness the transformation that happens behind the scenes and how each actor played a crucial role in bringing that character to life.

As I observed the rehearsal, I was captivated by how the students transformed under the stage lights. Their movements were deliberate, their voices carrying emotion to every corner of the auditorium. What truly fascinated me was all the preparations going on behind the scenes. I walked away with a deeper appreciation for the theater world.

I recommend that you research cosmetology schools if you want to specialize in theater, as you will also get exposed to handling wigs. Theater productions often require hairpieces, and if you can do both makeup and wigs, you're invaluable. I found this out first-hand. Unless you are a wig specialist or an SFX MUA, there might not be a reason for you to be hired as part of a live theater crew.

Having worked with Linda on both theater productions and film projects with her students, I can attest to her ability to make the on-set experience truly enriching with her hand-chosen costumes and beautifully designed outfits. I extend my sincere appreciation to her for granting me this invaluable opportunity.

## Film Department

In 2012, my passion for film was reignited when I had the privilege of collaborating with Tufts University's Film Department. This came about one day when Linda Girard was visiting my distribution company, Face Forward Inc, picking up her stage makeup order for her theater students, when she asked if I wanted to be introduced to her newest colleague, Professor Jennifer Burton. She was new in town and the professor of advanced film producing. Professor Burton was putting together a film production to give the students experience working on a film set with professionals. I told Linda that I would love to be introduced and to give Professor Burton my cell number and tell her I would love to help with her student film. I was thrilled to get a phone call the next day!

Meeting Professor Burton was an absolute honor. I felt as though I was in the right place at the right time when she extended an invitation for me to serve as the director of hair and makeup (HMU) for her seniors' upcoming film production. I embraced the opportunity without hesitation. This experience was deeply rewarding, as Professor Burton and her senior film students helped me make a life-changing decision to pursue a path within the film industry as an HMU artist.

That choice back in 2012 led to a long-standing, thirteen-year commitment with Professor Jennifer Burton and the Tufts University film students. Jennifer has graciously opened doors for me to work within the local independent film community, as several graduates went on to produce independent films or recommend me to executive producers.

### THE JOKER'S WILD

While discussing the unpredictable nature of connections, I've found tremendous value in a local costume enterprise called The Jokers Wild Costumes, located in Danvers, Massachusetts. Remarkably, this establishment has stood the test of time as a family-owned business. I can distinctly recall spending countless hours exploring this store wide-eyed when I was in cosmetology school, as the store was on my way home.

## Union Member: Traditional

To date, I've contributed to over a dozen independent films as well as several television commercials that were not affiliated with any union, placing them in the non-union category.

A union is an assembly of professionals united by a common interest, joining forces for the betterment of their trade. Eligibility criteria must be met, and dues are required for membership. Being part of a film union provides you with valuable perks, including access to health insurance, retirement plans, and job opportunities through their hiring and referral system. Membership also ensures improved working conditions, overtime pay, and legal representation in the event of disputes. It's called "collective bargaining," which is integral to the union, which allows MUAs to negotiate for better wages and hours. It actively negotiates contracts with film production companies on behalf of its members, providing long-term job security and stability.

Back in the day, the union system operated on the basis of seniority. At that time, juggling a marriage, three children, and managing a salon didn't allow me to be away from home for extended periods. Despite exploring membership in Local 798 in New York and beginning the paperwork, I eventually realized the impracticality of pursuing union membership. In the union realm, a choice between hair or makeup must be made, and the family circumstances at that time made it impossible for me to pursue membership.

You'll need to do your due diligence and research your local union. There are numerous requirements to join, and you can find them online.

## Non-Union: Freelancer

While the non-union status grants you the freedom to choose projects and work arrangements, it comes with the drawback of lacking access to union health insurance and retirement plans. Managing financial planning and retirement becomes an individual responsibility. For me, that was not a problem as my husband had our health insurance through his job.

It is important to recognize the competitive nature of the non-union market, given the substantial number of MUAs opting for this path. When hired by a non-union company, the responsibility falls on you to negotiate rates and working conditions. If you are working with a reputable film production company, then working conditions are a high priority for all involved.

Establishing connections early on as a freelancer was vital for me, given the film industry's reliance on referrals. I proactively shared my business information because I recognized early on the importance of networking. Assertively introducing myself and displaying my skills paved the way for future opportunities. The most valuable thing I can offer people when networking is my name and my reputation. I thought of it like I was planting a seed in my garden. Keep that in the back of your mind!

One of the key advantages of networking in the film industry is the opportunity to collaborate with like-minded professionals. For me, building relationships with fellow crew members has opened doors to numerous creative partnerships, for which I thank God. By collaborating with people who share your vision and passion, you will see how it elevates the quality of your work. I know this first-hand!

As a freelancer, networking will be your lifeline. You'll always move from one set to another. That means building solid, genuine connections with people is essential. A strong network will open doors to new opportunities, keep your calendar full, and bring in those referrals that often lead to long-term working relationships.

Let me share something important with you, especially if you're planning to work as a freelance MUA in film and television. In this industry, your reputation is everything. It's what gets you hired and keeps you working, project after project.

In 1987, I sold my first full-service beauty salon and embarked on my journey as a freelancer. I became known as an independent contractor. While being on my own provided me with the flexibility to manage my schedule, being my own boss was a huge responsibility.

Back then, communication didn't involve emails or texting; instead, business cards served as our primary means of contact, or we would usually use a landline phone that was attached to the wall. Yes, I'm revealing my age here. I vividly recall a moment on a film production when I forgot to pack my business cards and panicked. Improvising, I found a corner of the room and settled on the floor with my coffee. Manually, I transcribed my contact information eight times onto an eight-by-ten piece of paper, then cut it into eight card-sized pieces, and surprisingly, it did the trick!

As an independent freelance MUA, business cards were indispensable for my survival. Remember to avoid distributing your personal business card if you're part of a makeup company's team that hired you. I'll bet you a dollar that doing so will likely jeopardize your chances of being hired by them again. On the flip side, if you've been hired directly as a subcontractor by a production company, it's advisable to distribute your calling card to all film crew members.

In 1989, I told myself that if I didn't continue to promote what I wanted to do, then nobody else was going to do it for me. By that time, I was booking more hours in a photography studio and committing to commercial work with only a few small film jobs. It was the film work that I really wanted, but I did not want to go the union route.

So, I decided to start a "self-promoting campaign." I wrote a letter and sent it out to three dozen local film production companies, casting agencies, and film studios, letting them know what services I offered and that I was local. I focused on what services I provided and how I could be an asset to their future productions. About a week later, I got a letter from Paul, the manager of a local film production company, thanking me for contacting them and saying they would keep my name on file. That was a WOW moment for me! I still have that letter tucked away.

Even though I never worked directly for Paul, he let a few colleagues know about me, and I believe that is how I met Peter, who was a local photographer who specialized in black-and-white photos in the 1990s.

We exchanged my services for a small stipend covering gas, lunch, and eight-by-ten black-and-white headshots to add to my portfolio. Around that time, most casting agencies only required black-and-white headshots. It was a win-win situation.

## ABAREA MODELING SCHOOL

Another wonderful connection came my way in 1989, during the self-promotional campaign I launched. I had sent letters to owners of local modeling agencies and modeling training schools, knowing they often worked with HMU professionals. Four days after mailing those letters, I received a call from the director and owner of Abarea Modeling School, Dida Hagan. She told me she'd received my letter and asked if I would be interested in teaching her male and female students how to apply makeup and care for their skin. I said yes, and I started the following week. This was the start of a great connection and friendship. Thank you, Dida!

In the early 1990s, Dida and I did some exciting things together. She invited me to serve as a judge for both the Mrs. Massachusetts Pageant and the Mr. Male Model Pageant. That was a blast! Around the same time, she introduced me to a female photographer, and we worked out an exchange. I would provide hair and makeup services for her modeling clients, and in return, she gave me black-and-white eight-by-ten photographs of each model. I also exchanged my services with the models in return for their signed consent to use their eight-by-ten headshots for my business.

Those photographs were incredibly valuable to me at the time. Not only did they make my personal HMU portfolio stand out, but working with this photographer also gave me the opportunity to see first-hand how makeup responded to different lighting conditions in black-and-white photography.

## ADDITIONAL INSIGHTS

Here are a few additional insights that proved invaluable at the start of my makeup journey. It doesn't matter whether you are union or non-union. Immerse yourself in volunteering. Embrace the philosophy of "live and learn." By dedicating your time to assisting others, you gain the opportunity to absorb the knowledge of those you are supporting and create a mutually beneficial arrangement. I have never said no to a MUA or HMU artist who asked to volunteer to help me.

For those already established in the field as a cosmetologist, aesthetician, or MUA, consider crafting blog posts to showcase your expertise. Develop step-by-step tutorials that provide an in-depth look at the specific makeup looks you've created. If your business sells retail products, share comprehensive product reviews that highlight their effectiveness and include your personal recommendations. This not only enhances your credibility but also serves as an excellent strategy to boost sales and income. Additionally, don't overlook the importance of building a digital portfolio to showcase your finest work and attract potential clients from both the union and non-union worlds.

## Representing Yourself Professionally

Let's talk about another essential subject: representing yourself professionally. When you're on the job, how you present yourself and your team matter, so it's crucial to pay attention to this detail. Your dress attire should fit the assignment. If you're working on an outdoor film production, consider an appropriate outdoor wardrobe. You might find comfort in well-kept jeans, a proper shirt or sweatshirt, a makeup jacket, a makeup tool belt, and reliable sneakers.

Everyone has their own preferences when it comes to appearance, but one rule always applies: avoid looking disheveled. Keep it clean and simple. If you're working with a new production company, go for a slightly more conservative look; maybe black jeans, a polished top, and your makeup jacket.

As you get to know the production company and the film crew, you'll pick up on their style and expectations. Once you understand their norms, you can adapt your look accordingly without compromising your professionalism.

Adequate rest the night before is crucial, and it's advised not to wear any scented products on the day of filming. This precaution is especially important considering potential allergies among the film crew and actors. I have asthma and know first-hand how a scent can disrupt me … literally! I send an introduction letter to each actor before we meet on set, and I emphasize this point of non-scented products.

## 2  FINAL KEY THOUGHTS

- ☐ Enroll in specialized makeup training to meet the film industry's standards
- ☐ Keep up with the fast-paced industry through stamina and professionalism
- ☐ Stay flexible, build trust on set, and embrace the unexpected
- ☐ Choose structured union work or flexible non-union freelancing
- ☐ Expect long hours on a film production and off-set updates
- ☐ Dress professionally on the job; your appearance impacts your reputation

SCENE
GINGER
TAKE
1
HALF THE HISTORY -AC
JENN + URSULA BURTON
ALLIE HUMENUK
CAM
A+B
FPS
23.98

# CHAPTER 3

# Setting Up for Success

I can remember this scenario like it was yesterday. The familiar ringtone of my house phone echoed through the house as I ran to answer it. An unfamiliar voice crackled through the line, "Hey, it's Executive Producer Anne Alexander. I'm calling about the upcoming film you applied for! I love your resume, referrals, and portfolio work, and would like to offer you the job as my hair and makeup director."

Stunned, my mind raced in disbelief, wondering if this moment was real. After collecting myself from the shock, I eagerly responded, "Yes, I'd be honored to contribute to your film."

Without hesitation, I assured her of my availability, and I'm sure that she could hear the enthusiasm in my voice. With a sense of elation, I hung up the phone, still processing the gravity of the commitment I had just made. This was the moment I had been waiting for. It was time to chart the course for the journey ahead.

Long before I received that pivotal phone call, I understood the importance of having all my "ducks in a row." This chapter will walk you through what you'll need to do to prepare for your first professional film role as an MUA, from assembling portfolios to building your specialized kits and essential tools like release forms.

## Photo and Model Releases

If you lack professional photos for your first portfolio, you can utilize family members and friends. This is precisely what I did in the beginning of my career. Once I purchased my first salon, I had an endless list of clients who were eager to volunteer as models in exchange for a free haircut. First, they had to sign my model release form.

- ☐ Be professional from day one and capture close-up photos throughout the makeup application process, including before, during, and after.
- ☐ Take multiple shots from various angles, from the shoulders and closer. Include side profile views and full-faced views.
- ☐ Cultivate the habit of promptly documenting each person. By maintaining organized notes, you'll feel confident in reproducing any photo or film scene in the future.

## Models' Rights and Contributions

- ☐ I never assume my model will be comfortable with their photos being shared on social media or in my promotional materials. I respect their boundaries and preferences.
- ☐ Release forms set a clear expectation up front. It ensures that both of you will be on the same page about how their images may be used.
- ☐ Lawsuits are costly and time-consuming. Having a signed release form will prevent misunderstandings or disputes down the line. Don't skip this part!
- ☐ Using these releases demonstrates professionalism on your part. It shows that you take your work seriously and value each person.

Consulting a legal professional to ensure your release forms are drafted adequately for your business is crucial and worth the effort and expense. Trust me, it's far better to be safe than sorry. Release forms provide clarity, ensure mutual understanding, and safeguard against potential legal issues.

On this page is the photo and model release form I've successfully used for many years. Once the form has been signed, I give the model a copy of it or allow them to take a picture of it to keep on their phone.

## Photo and Model Release Form

I, _____________________ the undersigned, hereby grant my voluntary consent and authorization to Rhonda Cummings to serve as a model for purposes of demonstration, education, promotional, social media, and website purposes. I release Rhonda Cummings and Rc Makeup Artist, including its employees and associates, from any present or future claims, whether expressed or implied. Additionally, I relinquish all rights to photographs and videos taken by Rhonda Cummings and Rc Makeup Artist, allowing their use for demonstration, education, and promotional purposes. I confirm that all the information provided in this form is accurate to the best of my knowledge. By affixing my signature below, I acknowledge a complete understanding of the terms and confirm that no fees will be charged to me. The photos selected by Rhonda Cummings of Rc Makeup Artist will be considered my compensation for participating in this photography or video event.

Date: _________________ Name: _____________________________

E-mail: ________________________________________________________

Tel: ___________________________________________________________

Address: _______________________________ City: ________________

State: _______Zip: _____________________________________________

Witness: ___________________________________ Date: ___________

# Makeup Morgue Portfolio Books

Throughout my professional journey, I've created and maintained a series of meticulously organized morgue portfolio books. Each film I've worked on has its own dedicated book, neatly stored in a one-inch white three-ring binder. These books showcase the pre-production research I've done, the MUA designs I've prepared, and the steps and photographs of my actual work. This provides valuable visual references for future film projects. They serve not only as a creative archive but as a comprehensive catalog, packed with details. I often refer to these portfolios when planning new endeavors, ensuring continuity and inspiration. These books are essential tools, as they serve as my backup if a scene must be retaken at a future date. They are also excellent teaching tools for my MUA classes, plus they take me down memory lane repeatedly.

Upon completing each film project, I allocate a dedicated space for each white binder on my reference shelf for future consultations. Along the spine of each binder, I note the film title and date for easy identification. I diligently record detailed written notes in every book, establishing a valuable repository for future reference. These specialized books have evolved into my treasured library, cataloging both successful and unsuccessful creative experiments.

## INJURY MORGUE PORTFOLIO BOOK

As an SFX MUA, my work always begins with detailed communication with the executive producer. I ask critical questions to understand the nature of the injury being portrayed fully. Is it a superficial scratch or a deep wound? For something like a broken nose, I need specifics—was the impact frontal or from a side punch? Timing is equally important. I explore whether the injury is happening in real time or whether it's meant to show the passage of minutes, hours, or even a day later.

During one of my initial pre-production meetings for a film, I was tasked with creating an injury morgue portfolio book. This book showed images of various injuries, including cuts, scratches, black eyes, and the different stages of blood discoloration over time. The first six pages highlighted my own work, while the remaining six featured visuals sourced from online stock images, carefully printed and organized.

When I present this book for a project requiring an SFX MUA (Special Effects MUA), my primary objective is to educate the executive producer on the importance of accurate injury details and timing. Injuries involving blood, for instance, vary significantly depending on whether the wound is freshly bleeding or has dried over time. While the manuscript provides some guidance, it's up to the executive director to decide how the injury should ultimately appear. These decisions directly influence how you'll approach your SFX MUA designs.

Visual aids are essential during your first pre-production meeting. They not only help convey the possibilities but also ensure that everyone on the team has a clear vision of the desired outcome. This collaborative approach will allow you to create injuries that are both realistic and aligned with the film's narrative, enhancing the story's authenticity.

## FACIAL HAIR MORGUE PORTFOLIO BOOK

When I'm tasked with enhancing or adding to an actor's facial hair, my go-to resource is my trusted "Facial Hair Morgue Portfolio Book." It's an invaluable tool for projects set in specific historical periods. If I'm asked to showcase period work from, say, the 1800s to 1910, or if the film is set in 1972 and the main character sports a mustache and sideburns, I know exactly where to turn. I simply pull examples from my past film work; all carefully preserved in my three-ring white film binders.

I always immerse myself in research about the film's era, ensuring

I have accurate reference photos from the exact year or period. This attention to detail allows me to bring authenticity to every film production, no matter what the time frame.

## AGING MORGUE PORTFOLIO BOOK

One of the resources I rely on heavily is my "Aging Morgue Portfolio Book." For instance, if a forty-year-old male actor is cast to play a character in his sixties, I use this book to guide the transformation. The process often involves aging the actor and adding gray and white to his beard, sideburns, and mustache. However, a critical question always arises: what is the precise target age for the character? To ensure accuracy, I thoroughly review the script and the executive producer's notes. If the character is described as a man in his sixties, I know I need to narrow down the age range. Should he look like someone in his early sixties or late sixties?

If I initially aged the actor to sixty years old but later learn that the executive producer envisioned him at sixty-eight, adjustments are relatively simple. However, if I aged him to sixty-eight, I may need to remove and reapply the makeup entirely, including altering the gray and white in his facial hair. Instead of making assumptions, I will address this directly with the executive producer during our pre-production meeting. Having visual aids during these discussions is vital.

## BLACK-AND-WHITE MUA MORGUE PORTFOLIO BOOK

In the early stages of my career, circa the late 1980s, I crafted my inaugural "Black-and-White Makeup Morgue Portfolio Book" while collaborating with a photographer who specialized in black-and-white headshots for actors. This portfolio remained shelved until 2014, when I was enlisted to collaborate with Tufts University Theater and Film students on a live stage rendition of the life of a famous 1920s Asian female actor. Executive Director and Producer, Cinthia Chen's vision involved recreating the live stage narrative in color and having it filmed in black-and-white, plus hundreds of students in the audience to support this event.

On the day of the live stage filming, you could not only see the excitement in the audience, but you could also feel it both behind the scenes and on the stage during setup. The 1920s costumes worn by the cast were remarkably accurate, closely mirroring those used in the original film remake. I was tasked with overseeing the preparation of two key actors' makeup and was responsible for ensuring their wigs stayed in place. One of them portrayed the youthful eighteen-year-old actor, while the other embodied the forty-five-year-old version of the iconic woman.

Before commencing with the makeup and hair preparations, I ventured onto the stage to assess the lighting. Positioning myself where the actors would stand and sit, I thoroughly examined the setup. Directly behind the designated actor area, on the back wall of the stage, hung a two-story white screen designed to project live filming in black-and-white in real time.

To my surprise, I soon encountered a glitch. I knew the entire production was being filmed in black-and-white as if it were a remake of the 1929 movie, but there was going to be a live audience. Now, faced with a pivotal decision, I pondered whether to apply makeup to the actors for the intended black-and-white filming, as initially planned, or tailor it for the live theater production.

After encountering several challenges and feeling a bit frustrated, I approached the director of photography, seeking his advice. His initial reaction was one of bewilderment, but after a moment of contemplation, he exclaimed, "I have an idea!"

He dashed off and returned with a peculiar eight-by-ten foil that possessed a translucent quality. The foil appeared slightly distorted, having been crumpled and then carefully unfolded. Without hesitation, he affixed the crinkled foil over the camera lens. To our astonishment, the resulting imagery closely resembled the authentic 1929 film, complete with crackling lines. This ingenious solution resolved my query. I opted to enhance the actors' stage makeup specifically for projection, ensuring a vivid display for the live audience without affecting the black-and-white filming.

This experience became a valuable lesson for both of us. It was remarkable how a seemingly insignificant eight-by-ten piece of crumpled foil became the savior of the day for me. After this revelation, I proceeded backstage to prepare the two female actors for their stage roles. Meanwhile, the sounds of people entering the theater signaled the approaching live performance.

Like the crumpled foil that was handy, I'm always unsure about what I'll need that I haven't planned for. So, I tend to bring everything but the kitchen sink. One thing is certain: effective pre-production is crucial for staying sharp. Having the right makeup tools, equipment, and products is essential for enduring long hours, hot lights, and unpredictable weather.

## Professional MUA Kits

Investing in tools, supplies, and equipment is essential. Be prepared to make this financial commitment. Start by prioritizing the basics, such as acquiring makeup cases to organize and safeguard your products, tools, and equipment. These cases don't have to be extravagant, but what matters most is their durability during transportation.

As the years went on, my makeup kits got bigger and better! For every job, I would allocate 15 percent of my income to replace and purchase new materials and 25 percent toward my end-of-the-year taxes, as I was a sole proprietor.

Reflecting on my own experience, my first traveling makeup kit for my first film job was a plastic toolbox purchased by my husband at Sears

Hardware Store in 1978, shortly after we got married. Surprisingly, it turned out to be a reliable choice, and to this day, it serves as one of my special effects MUA kits.

This two-foot-tall toolbox was squared, light gray in color, and featured a spacious top drawer with multiple sections and six bottom drawers capable of holding a substantial amount of makeup. There was a slight hiccup; I had no makeup to fill the toolbox for my first job. So, off I went to the local department store and drugstore to purchase affordable makeup. At that time, I couldn't afford expensive professional palettes or high-quality brushes, but it was a crucial step in getting started. My first job went so well that it led to two more small filming jobs.

## CAMOUFLAGE MAKEUP KIT

My camouflage makeup kit is always on set with me. It is my wonder kit! Here's another noteworthy scenario: how do you handle a situation where a character in the script doesn't have a tattoo, but the actor portraying them does?

The solution involves using a foundation with a high pigment concentration, such as fifty percent camouflage makeup. Additionally, it requires a thorough understanding of proper layering techniques with the correct makeup sponges and the application of specialized setting powders to effectively prevent the tattoo from bleeding through. The selected setting powder should be resistant to both heat and muscle movements, as well as waterproof, to ensure that the tattoo remains covered throughout the entire day. This has always been proven to be my gold star product.

## SKIN CARE KIT

As your business expands, you'll find yourself adding more items to all your specialty kits. Essential additions will include items for preparing the actor's skin before applying makeup. Often, the actor's skin condition remains unknown until the day of their scene. To address this, you must maintain a skin care kit containing a variety of facial moisturizers and lip moisturizers, as well as a primer with silicone (ensuring it is non-reflective). Additionally, carry makeup cleansers to remove the actor's makeup at the end of each filming day.

Don't forget to include travel-sized shaving cream and razors in case they are needed before the makeup application. I prefer them to shave up to the evening before their call time. There's nothing worse than an actor who is spot bleeding from shaving an hour before he arrives in my chair.

## ACTOR'S ON-LOCATION KITS

Once the actor's makeup is completed, you can transfer the brushes and all products used on them into a clear plastic container that has their name on it for touch-ups. This will become the actor's on-location makeup kit.

When deciding how to organize and store the kits, I prefer utilizing a variety of backpacks and fanny packs, as well as wearing clothing with ample pockets. One of my preferred backpacks is a baby's diaper bag. It features a convenient side compartment for storing makeup wipes and numerous small compartments, including a waterproof one suitable for holding an ice pack, particularly useful in hot weather.

If I'm filming outdoors in a wooded area, I'll pack a long rope and clothespins. This allows me to hang up essential items such as predesigns, photos, and the daily call sheet by stringing rope and using clothespins to secure the items.

## YOUR TRAVELING OFFICE KIT

When you're on the go, having a reliable traveling office kit can keep you organized and ready for anything. Keep it compact so it fits easily into any of your larger kits or cases. Include a black pen for professional notes and a red pen for marking or underlining important details. A small stapler is a must; make sure to tuck a few extra staples into a small envelope so you're never without the ability to bind documents.

For quick fixes or attaching papers, carry a roll of scotch tape; it always comes in handy. Use a bright yellow highlighter to emphasize key sections of documents, and pack both black and red permanent markers for labeling or writing that needs to last. Finally, don't forget a pad of yellow-lined paper for jotting down ideas, drafting notes, or sketching quick plans. This simple kit helps keep your mobile workspace functional and efficient wherever you are.

## PERSONAL SURVIVAL KIT

You'll want to get into the habit of bringing your own personal survival kit. It's always smart to include an extra set of clothing because you never know what the day will bring. The daily call sheet will give you the rundown on the weather, so check it before heading out. If you're filming indoors with a green-screen setup, keep in mind that you can't walk on that specialized flooring with regular shoes. Be sure to have socks on hand for those moments when you need to step in for touch-ups during filming.

Pack essential hygiene items to help you make it through the day. Think of a portable toothbrush, travel-sized deodorant, any medications you may need, your phone charger, and, if you're bringing your laptop, don't forget the charger for that, too. These items can really save you when the day gets long.

I always take a reusable water container and refill it with the bottled water provided on set. The production company will have a designated craft and catering area with daily meals and snacks. You'll find the location for that listed right on your daily call sheet.

### FIRST AID KIT

You're not required to bring a first aid kit to the set; there will be one available. Still, it's a good habit to carry a few basics like bandages, antiseptics, and anti-itch cream. Building that kind of self-reliance will serve you well in this industry.

If you're heading to an outdoor location, don't forget bug repellent. It's a must. When you're filming outside in the heat, bring along a compact cooler bag with reusable freezer packs. It's not just for keeping your water cold; it also protects your makeup creams and pencil liners from melting in the heat.

## Traveling with MUA Cases and Tools

A crucial aspect to consider regarding your makeup cases is to keep them with you when traveling in a vehicle. When I travel by airplane, I make it a practice to send my cases and tools to a secure location at least two weeks in advance. This proactive approach is necessary because I often utilize special effects makeup, which airlines typically prohibit as carry-on items.

The post office is my preferred shipping method for my makeup cases and tools due to its cost-effectiveness, tracking capabilities, and insurance options. This way, I can monitor the delivery status and, in the unfortunate event of loss, have sufficient time to replace the contents. Given the unpredictability of situations, it's essential to stay prepared.

Reflecting on an experience, I recall a day when I was hired as the HMU director on a television commercial that was being shot in two different locations in one day. After completing the morning shoot, we packed up and drove to our second filming site, a four-hour drive away.

Upon arrival, we learned that one of the two supply vans was in a car accident and was two hours away from us. Unfortunately, my makeup cases were in the van involved in the accident.

Once I got word of the accident, I encouraged the executive producer not to disrupt the scheduled plans, expressing my commitment to making it work. However, I needed a quick solution, so I asked all the female crew members to empty out their pocketbooks and makeup bags. Luckily, it was a success! Thank goodness the afternoon scenes didn't require real close-ups or special effects, as all the intricate make-up and filming work for close-ups had been completed at the first location that morning.

I was relieved, and so was the entire film crew, that we didn't have to wait for my makeup cases. By the time the cases finally arrived, we were halfway through filming. Everyone was genuinely appreciative of how I handled the situation, and that memory stuck with each of them. It all worked out, and now we share laughs about it whenever we meet! Since then, I've had the opportunity to collaborate with each of them on separate projects.

## MAKEUP BRUSH KITS

For each day on set, you should tailor your kits to match the details outlined in the daily call sheet (refer to Chapter 5). Consider the specific scenes each actor is in and the filming location. Your makeup brush kits will become the cornerstone of your work. In film production, paying attention to every detail is crucial, and using the correct brushes gives you greater control and precision during application.

You'll want to build a collection that includes both natural and synthetic brushes in a variety of sizes, shapes, and bristle textures. This variety helps you achieve seamless blending and a polished final look. It takes time to truly understand what each brush can and can't do, so keep learning and experimenting.

Brush preferences are highly personal, and each one has its own unique function. You'll likely find yourself relying heavily on synthetic brushes, especially when working with special effects. Don't forget to include essentials like metal spatulas, two-inch by three-inch metal plates to hold products, disposable mascara and lip brushes, and plenty of latex-free disposable makeup wedges.

Another key factor to consider when choosing your brushes is the *ingredients or medium* you'll be working with. Take time to understand the composition of your creams, liquids, pastes, powders, emulsions, and adhesives. This knowledge helps you refine your application techniques and make better decisions on set. Be sure that your products are formulated to withstand being exposed to hot lights and long film hours. Know what these ingredients can and cannot do and always follow the manufacturer's instructions.

## NATURAL BRISTLE BRUSHES

Once I discovered the magic of natural bristle brushes, I finally felt like a true artist! It's essential to understand how these brushes work best with your various makeup products before even picking one up.

My collection includes a range of sizes and shapes, and I use them primarily for dry powder applications. My go-to is the dome-shaped natural bristle fluff brush because it holds a generous amount of powder, making it incredibly versatile. My personal favorite is the angled brush. Its unique shape gives me excellent control and precision, making it a reliable tool in my kit. I used to buy a dozen fluff brushes at a time and give them "haircuts" to mimic an angled brush. It was a budget-friendly way to expand my collection and customize brushes to suit my needs.

## SYNTHETIC BRISTLE BRUSHES

Your synthetic bristle brushes will likely become some of your favorite tools for applying creams, aqua colors, and special effects. These brushes offer remarkable precision, especially when defining detailed areas like the brow line, eyes, or lips. Made from man-made materials such as nylon or polyester fibers, synthetic brushes lack a cuticle, giving them a firmer texture—ideal for accuracy and control.

When selecting the right synthetic bristle brush, consider the size of the area you're working on and the effect you want to achieve. Ask yourself whether a dome-shaped, oval, round, flat, or angled brush will best suit your needs. They're also essential for working with actors who have sensitivities or allergies to animal hair, ensuring that every application is safe and comfortable. I once worked with an actor who had a latex allergy, and I had to create a custom kit and work in a separate room to ensure their safety and comfort.

## CLEANING MUA BRUSHES

Maintaining the cleanliness of your makeup brushes is an essential post-work ritual. It's a daily task you can't afford to skip, as neglecting it can lead to regret. Don't give in to the temptation to toss your dirty brushes into a bag, thinking you'll clean them later. That's a surefire way to damage the bristles. Instead, treat your brushes with care and affection, and store them just as gently.

When cleaning your natural bristle brushes, use an alcohol-based brush cleaner. Lay each brush flat on paper towels and spray both sides thoroughly. Wipe it clean and repeat the process until there's no excess color remaining.

For your **synthetic brushes**, you can also use an alcohol-based brush cleanser. Start by immersing them in a cup of brush cleanser. Then rinse with clean water, repeat if needed. After cleaning both types of brushes, gently squeeze out any excess water, reshape the bristles, and lay them flat on a paper towel to dry overnight.

# High-Definition Foundations

High-definition (HD) foundations are specially formulated to meet the demands of today's high-definition filming technology, which captures images with exceptional clarity and detail. While specific formulations may vary between brands and products, there are some common characteristics and ingredients often found in these foundations. Many of these products utilize silicone-based formulas.

Silicone provides a smooth, lightweight texture that glides onto the skin effortlessly, creating a flawless finish. I love using a silicone-based foundation as it helps to blur imperfections and create a soft effect. Often, it contains finely milled micro-pigments. These pigments help to even out skin tone and provide seamless coverage without appearing cakey on camera.

High-definition foundations are typically oil-free and non-comedogenic, meaning they won't clog pores or contribute to breakouts. This is important for maintaining the appearance of clear, blemish-free skin under the scrutiny of high-definition cameras. They are designed to last for hours of filming, stay in place, and are available in various mediums. I personally prefer a matte finish to control shine and create a smooth, natural-looking complexion on camera.

# Face Powders

Face powders are a must-have in your kit because they help mattify shine on an actor's face and set their makeup. If you understand color theory, you can customize hundreds of shades and produce various tones to create a wide range of translucent setting face powders.

When you're using high-definition foundations, make sure to pair them with high-definition face powders. However, if the actor is exposed to water, never use a powdered product. In that case, your best choice is a waterproof fixer spray.

Below is a list of items you'll find in my makeup kits. I like to use color palettes that include twenty-four different colors to create hundreds of colors and tones. All my products exclude reflective ingredients unless specifically requested. I do use reflective products for numerous live events when requested.

- ☐ **Cleansers and Moisturizers:** I carry a variety to customize.
- ☐ **Facial Primers:** My choice for a primer must have a silicone base.
- ☐ **Foundations:** I have a case just for liquid and cream foundations.
- ☐ **Face Powders:** I customize from over a dozen shades and tones.
- ☐ **Cream Products:** Used for eyes, cheeks, contour, and highlighting.
- ☐ **Eyebrows and Eyeliners:** You can't skimp on these; I have every color in pencil, solids, and liquid.
- ☐ **Mascara:** I utilize both cake and liquid mascara in black and brown, and I prefer waterproof mascara unless there is an issue with the actor.
- ☐ **Lipliners:** I carry a variety of colors in matte, which is non-reflective. Lip gloss is a no-no because, due to its reflective properties, it will reflect off the camera.
- ☐ **Lipstick:** My twenty-four-color lip palette will give me all the colors I'll ever need, and if it doesn't, I'll custom blend one.

## ADDITIONAL TOOLS YOU'LL FIND IN MY CASES

- ☐ Clear nail color, polish remover, and nail files
- ☐ Clear zippy bags and trash bags
- ☐ My "office in a jar" consists of a pen, a highlighter, tape, and a small stapler
- ☐ A backpack and fanny pack

- ☐ Disposable latex-free gloves; make sure you get your correct size
- ☐ It's always helpful to have a small folding table and two extension cords
- ☐ I always take two pencil sharpeners with me in case one breaks
- ☐ Full and half-size clothing capes are used to cover the actor's costume
- ☐ An umbrella and raincoat if the weather predicts rain or snow; I will also store all my equipment in waterproof bags or in my metal cases
- ☐ In the winter: warm clothing, a waterproof jacket, boots, a hat, and gloves
- ☐ In the summer, I never know if the temperature in the room will be cold (air conditioner) or warm (no air conditioner), so I bring a mini fan that is run by batteries to cool things down (take extra batteries), and I also always carry an extra set of summer clothes with me, as you can get pretty heated up in a room with a full film crew
- ☐ I have a personal bag that consists of an extra pair of eyeglasses, a toothbrush, toothpaste, personal items, my makeup, and snack bars

Pack everything the day before and get a good night's sleep!

## HAIR KIT

For cosmetologists who are handling both the hair and makeup departments, here's a glimpse into my hair kit essentials. If the actor requires a wig, I include the wig, wig forms, wig combs, wig brushes, and t-pins to secure the wig to a wig form. The contents of my hair kit are tailored to the specific hair services needed each day. All hair color changes and haircuts for actors are completed before the actual filming.

When preparing my hair kit, I streamline things by transferring larger bottles of hair products into smaller ones to optimize space. The essentials include a non-reflective shampoo, a hair conditioner, and a hair styling gel. I rarely use any form of hairspray to avoid unwanted reflections in the camera, and, notably, I use pumps exclusively rather than aerosol spray cans.

Below are the minimum products and tools you'll find in my hair kit.

- ☐ **Hairbrushes and Combs:** A variety of different sizes and shapes.
- ☐ **Hair Pins:** All colors and shades of light, medium, and dark in my kit.
- ☐ **Hair Tools:** Scissors (2), hairdryers (2), curling irons, and flat irons.
- ☐ **Hair Elastics:** Coated elastics in a variety of colors, sizes, and widths.
- ☐ **Hair Products:** For styling and achieving the finished look.
- ☐ **Hair Wig Nets:** You will need to match the wig color exactly.
- ☐ **Hair Nets:** Are thinner than a conventional hair wig net.

I keep several hair nets with me, even when I don't have to apply a wig. I use them to hold hair in place, for updos, or to keep a ponytail nice and tight. I carry every color: white, gray, blonde, medium red, light-medium-dark brown, and black.

## TEMPORARY HAIR RINSES

Temporary hair rinses are an absolute must in your kit. They're your go-to solution for scenes involving progressive aging or de-aging. You can find them at most beauty supply stores. These products are colored liquids that come in a wide range of colors and shades that you apply directly to the hair roots and comb through. Shake the bottle frequently, and don't hesitate to custom-blend shades as needed. Avoid diluting these products with water, as it will change the color and tone.

Temporary hair rinses usually last just one or two washes, making them ideal for temporary transformations on the actor. Understanding base colors is crucial when mixing these rinses to achieve the perfect shade or when applying them to white hair. If the result is too dark, it's back to washing and starting over. Preparation and precision are key to achieving the final look.

## TEMPORARY HAIR PAINT

When an actor's aging process is written into the script, you must know the precise age of the character at that point in the story. Are they just beginning to show signs of aging, or are they much further along? These details matter. Temporary hair paint is an essential tool in your kit when aging actors for their roles. This liquid has a thicker consistency, making it ideal for creating realistic effects. You'll apply it using a synthetic brush, carefully painting onto the hairline or facial hair.

For subtle effects, hand-painting white, light gray, or dark gray streaks into the hairline and blending them naturally between strands yields the best results. This process requires precision and a thorough understanding of the pre-production plans and the character's development. Preparation is everything. Without a clear roadmap for each actor and every scene, your results can easily miss the mark.

When you're adding colors to the hair, stay laser-focused. Once you're three-quarters of the way, ask the first assistant producer to arrange for the executive producer to review the progress. You'll have direct access to the first assistant director who works closely with the executive producer. Whether it's a quick FaceTime or an in-person check, you'll get an immediate response, either a "Perfect, I love it," or a request for a subtle adjustment to make the actor appear slightly younger or older.

### MEN'S ELECTRIC SHAVER

A men's electric shaver is another must-have tool in your kit. Choose one with attachments to trim facial hair, beards, mustaches, and necklines for a cleaner, more polished look. Don't forget to pack the charger and extra batteries.

I always carry two sets of clippers. If one dies, I have a backup ready. I do the same with my hairdryers, irons, and scissors. Early in my career on a film set, my hairdryer suddenly stopped working. After taking a moment to calm down, I improvised by using the wall-mounted hand dryer in the ladies' room to dry the actor's hair. It worked and taught me a valuable lesson: always be prepared.

## Color Theory: Black-and-White

Color theory revolves around three primary colors: blue, red, and yellow. Combining equal parts of these primaries results in brown, which serves as the foundational element for all other colors. Mixing them in varying proportions produces secondary colors, such as purple (blue and red), orange (red and yellow), and green (blue and yellow). Tertiary colors emerge when secondary colors are combined.

As I've previously mentioned, you do not need an arsenal of color palettes at your disposal. Once you understand basic color theory, you can mix and match colors. This chapter is not a color theory course. When you first start to build your makeup kits, don't buy singular or dual compacts when it comes to cosmetic powders and creams.

Get a six-color palette, at minimum, plus a black-and-white color separately. This way, you can custom-blend and make hundreds of different colors and tones. I'll use dark blue as an example. I always use an equation of ten parts, which gives me an abundance of color shades from light to dark.

When you add white to any color, it will become much lighter.

| | |
|---|---|
| 1 white | 9 blue |
| 2 white | 8 blue |
| 3 white | 7 blue |
| 4 white | 6 blue |
| 5 white | 5 blue |
| 6 white | 4 blue |
| 7 white | 3 blue |
| 8 white | 2 blue |
| 9 white | 1 blue |

What happens when you change the white, above, to black? When you add black to any color, it will add depth and deepen the color. To create a broader palette, you can add three colors to this equation. Add one part black, one part white, and eight parts blue. You get the drift? I always think of it as a ten-part equation. The colors are exponential once you understand the difference between a color tone and a color shade.

I can't stress enough that you need to understand basic color theory, as this will help you expand your makeup palettes beyond your wildest dreams. It will also help to reduce the number of color palettes you have to carry with you, and best of all, it will save you money. I first learned about color theory in cosmetology school from hair coloring classes and deepened my understanding with advanced hair coloring courses once I graduated.

## Chiaroscuro

Consider that your upcoming film project is being filmed in black-and-white. Now you're entering the realm of chiaroscuro, but what is it? It's a technical term used by artists to denote the deliberate use of stark contrasts between dark and light within the black-and-white spectrum.

Undertaking projects involving black-and-white photography or filming presents distinct challenges.

I can remember as a teenager sitting outside in my backyard with a sketch book and charcoal pencils. I'd observe how the sunlight would hit the huge white birch tree or the many other trees within the half-acre of our property, and draw my interpretation of what I had just witnessed, concentrating on the highlights hitting the trees and the contour of shadows. My Dad's cherry tree was another of my favorite subjects to draw. In fact, my mother told me that when I was twelve years old, I gave my Dad's big, beautiful cherry tree a haircut! She knew then that I was going to be a hairdresser.

## 3 FINAL KEY THOUGHTS

- ☐ Always show up prepared, looking professional, with proper paperwork in place.
- ☐ Keep your makeup kits organized, labeled, and stored safely to maintain quality.
- ☐ Sanitize tools and workspaces consistently throughout the day.
- ☐ Clean habits and reliability build a strong, lasting reputation.
- ☐ Use photos and character files to maintain flawless continuity.
- ☐ Follow etiquette by silencing or powering down your phone when required.
- ☐ Master color theory to match tones, correct flaws, and elevate your work.

REV WAR
ROLL
SCENE
TAKE
A 01
514 - LUCY
2
Director
ALEX
Camera
STEVE SHERRICK

CHAPTER 4

# Pre-Production

## Secrets to Crafting a Makeup Team

I've learned that crafting a professional makeup team is an art. This team becomes the heartbeat of the production, and every member plays an important role in bringing the manuscript to life through their artistry. If you're hoping to join a team, such as mine, understand that I start by looking at your educational background first and then your portfolio. These aren't just boxes that I check off; they lay the foundation for a strong relationship.

Your portfolio doesn't just tell me or a producer where you've been; it shows us what you're capable of doing. It's more than just a collection of photos; it's your voice, your imagination, and your technical skills all in one place. A great portfolio might open the door, but *you* are the one who walks through it.

We want to see your full range of skills and, most importantly, your ability to adapt to different styles and challenges. If your work aligns with the vision of the film project you've applied for, and your attitude reflects collaboration and passion, then chances are, you're exactly what we're looking for.

The real magic begins once you enter the room for your interview. In that room, your passion, dedication, and creative spark can leave a lasting impression. This is your opportunity to show how you bring characters to life and how you interpret a manuscript.

## EXPECTATIONS

Flexibility is a non-negotiable trait for any makeup artist I hire. Film sets are unpredictable environments; schedules change, actors evolve, and creative choices can shift in the blink of an eye. I look for professionals who are not only skilled but also adaptable individuals who can think on their feet and adjust their process without compromising quality. They must stay calm under pressure, meet tight deadlines, and produce looks that meet my expectations.

Another cornerstone of my criteria is attention to detail. Makeup isn't just about making someone look good on camera; it's about telling a story through their appearance. A well-designed makeup look can tell the audience who a character is before they utter a single word. When I assign an MUA to a specific actor, I need them to study my designs and execute them flawlessly. Whether we're talking about the subtle aging of a character, aging across decades, or the carefully placed bruising on an action hero, every element matters. The smallest detail can make the biggest difference, and the best MUAs know this instinctively.

As part of the team, you're doing more than applying makeup; you're helping to shape the story. Every brushstroke, every detail you design adds to the authenticity and believability as it unfolds in front of the camera. Your work doesn't just support the manuscript; it enhances it!

Over the years, I've been fortunate to collaborate with many MUAs who also excel in cosmetology and wig applications. This skill set is a game-changer, especially on smaller productions where resources may be stretched thin, and flexibility is paramount.

Choosing the right makeup team isn't just about talent; it's about trust, collaboration, and shared vision. They are a group of diverse professionals who are artists who breathe life into characters. Together, we craft stories that linger long after the credits roll, and for me, that is the ultimate reward.

# Navigating Through a Manuscript

You must read and understand the manuscript, as you will be expected to immerse yourself fully in the story, not just skim for cues or scene numbers. You need to break down each character's journey and anticipate how their appearance evolves throughout the film. Are they worn down by hardship? Does their confidence show through a more polished look? Is a scar silently telling a deeper story? These are the details you need to pick up on, as they will elevate your makeup designs from simply functional to truly unforgettable.

I still vividly remember my first independent film project. It was then that I truly understood that being a MUA for film was so much more than just applying makeup. It was about helping tell a story, enhancing each character's journey. Looking back on my own journey, I see that every project, no matter how straightforward or complicated it appeared, unfolded like a storybook before my eyes. These manuscripts weren't just stacks of paper; they were vibrant blueprints, crafted to bring a vision to life through visual storytelling.

In this role, *you* are the captain of the makeup ship. It's your responsibility to research, develop, and execute the look the film's visionaries hired you to bring to life. Every choice you make must align with the story and serve the characters' journey.

Skipping any step in this process isn't just risky, it's a mistake that can cost you future opportunities. Success in this industry depends on your preparation, your ability to collaborate, and your relentless dedication to excellence. And for you, just like it is for me, it all starts with the manuscript.

## THE PROCESS

When I read a manuscript, I don't just see dialogue and direction; I see a cinematic adventure waiting to unfold. My first read is always about immersion. I never use a pen or notepad to take notes during this initial read; in fact, I strongly believe you shouldn't either. If necessary, sit on your hands! Instead, I find a quiet, distraction-free space where I can fully absorb the story. This ritual is crucial to my process. Neglecting to read the manuscript thoroughly will be noticed by all the executive directors at the pre-production meeting.

After the first read, I'll embark on a second round, this time armed with a pen and paper. During this focused reading, I'll note the details of each character's description, personality, social standings, the year, the season, indoor or outdoor, time of day, and other elements that stand out.

Once I've finished, I carefully review my notes and arrange them to align with the manuscript. Then, I organize everything into a white three-ring binder. This approach mirrors the process of creating a morgue reference book, ensuring my observations are well-organized and accessible.

With the executive producer's approval, I provide each member of my team with a copy of the manuscript. They are expected to familiarize themselves with this before our first pre-production meeting. These pieces of paper serve as a guiding compass that translates the narrative onto the screen. Without it, every member of the film crew would be lost in a sea of uncertainty.

A great example of this is when I read the manuscript and learn that water will be involved in a scene. My radar goes up, and the questions are written down. Will the actor be outside in the rain or conveying emotions through tears of joy or sorrow? Perhaps they'll be engaging in activities like swimming or sweating profusely while running a mara-thon. Understanding these nuances within the manuscript dictates the makeup products you will apply to the actor for each scene. Immediately, I will reach for waterproof makeup. By considering these factors, I can effectively tailor the makeup application to suit the demands of each scene and character.

Before the first pre-production meeting, I use my binder to clearly and effectively present my questions. Timing is everything during this meeting, so being well-prepared is crucial. This small detail not only adds a polished appearance but also signals to the executive producer that I am organized, meticulous, and ready to contribute. They notice these things because they want to see that their film crew is prepared and capable of handling the demands of a live film production. This structured approach has, and still does, serve me well in demonstrating professionalism and earning trust in my role.

In the initial pre-production meeting, it's crucial to incorporate actor-related details. Your primary role in this first meeting is to listen attentively and absorb information. Exercising prudence is key during this initial gathering, and you should always refrain from proposing alterations right away. If your opinion is sought, don't hesitate to share it. I've learned that being valued from your perspective is an asset and a fantastic opportunity to share your experience and vision. With every meeting you attend, you'll gain more access to the "laws of the film world," which gives you more confidence to engage.

## Collaborating with the Costume Designer

The role of the makeup director demands a close and intricate partnership with the costume designer. This collaboration is one of the most rewarding aspects of my work because it brings characters to life on screen in a truly cohesive way. I've been privileged to work with the talented costume designer, Toni Elliott, for twelve years. From the start, we have immersed ourselves in sharing reference images and pictures to ensure our visions align. Each of us brings our unique expertise to the table, working together to create a unified look.

Effective communication with the costume designer is essential, not just during pre-production, but throughout the entire filming process. This collaboration fuels a creative synergy where we bounce ideas off each other to craft visual designs. Inspiration often flows between us, even on set, pushing our individual contributions to new heights. Before shooting begins each day, we check in with one another to discuss any adjustments or tweaks necessary for the day's scenes, ensuring that every detail is flawless and consistent.

Drawing from my wealth of past experiences, I have cultivated a profound appreciation for the precision and details required during the pre-production phase, which makes the production phase go as scheduled. I understand the pivotal role I play in collaborating closely with the costume designer, a partnership essential to achieving a cohesive vision of each character's complete on-screen appearance. This collaboration ensures that every detail is tailored to the manuscript. It helps me to achieve a comprehensive understanding of each character's total appearance. My preparation involves going beyond surface details. I'll conduct a thorough inquiry to ensure I fully understand the requirements, which is vital to understanding the unique demands of each setting, allowing me to craft solutions that align with the film's production vision and contribute meaningfully to its overall success.

## Analyzing Characters Through the Manuscript

When you begin analyzing a character in the manuscript, your approach should be meticulous and thorough. Reading and fully understanding the script's intricacies is the first step toward visualizing the character. Start by analyzing their background, motivations, and personality traits. Understanding their journey is essential to bringing them to life visually.

Next, carefully observe and study the actor's facial features, especially in documentary work. This attention to detail helps you capture subtle nuances and expressions that add authenticity. From there, identify the specific traits that make this character unique. It could be a physical feature, a mannerism, or a particular quirk. In documentaries, you may even need to alter the actor's facial features or hairline to reflect the real-life person more accurately. Whatever the case, stay rooted in authenticity and use your creative skills to enhance believability on screen.

Finally, through practice and refinement of drawings, you'll be prepared to make the character's appearance reflect their personality and role in the story, completing the intricate process of character development.

Here's a scenario from a film I was working on a few years ago that was set in the spring of 1910 in the streets of New York City. According to the manuscript, the male character was a handsome thirty-eight-year-old man with a slim build who was six feet two inches tall with a clean 1910s hairstyle. The manuscript continued to inform me that he was fashionably dressed in a three-piece black suit, black shiny shoes, a white shirt, a white bow tie, and a black top hat. He would also be sporting a fashionable mustache and sideburns.

When I started researching, I found several facial looks for the male character's age that aligned with what I imagined the executive producer was looking for. My designs showed that the actor's mustache would extend three-quarters of an inch past the corner of his mouth and curl up. Each sideburn would start from the top of the ear and continue just below the corner of his mouth, with very bushy sideburns along his jawline. This was my number one vision I had for this character. I also did a copy and paste report with several other male facial looks from the 1910s era. At the first pre-production meeting, I asked the executive producer if he had reference photos for the 1910s look he had envisioned. Indeed, he did, and I wasn't too far off in my assessment.

In addition to the above steps, I read into the character's occupation, recognizing its pivotal role in shaping the actor's appearance. This particular character was the president of a bank in New York City and was among New York City's most well-known families. This is where the manuscript will voice who and what the character will portray. Understanding their profession helps to craft a visual representation that resonates with the audience's perception. Furthermore, I explore the character's personal style, discerning whether their appearance leans towards the stylish or the average, or whether they simply don't prioritize their outward presentation. This attention to detail ensures that every aspect of the character's visual portrayal aligns seamlessly with their narrative and personality.

On the day of filming this scene, I recreated the exact look previously discussed with the executive producer and costume designer for this actor. On set, I scheduled time to shave his chin to match the period's fashionable style. Leading up to this, I had been in close contact with this actor. I instructed him to grow out his facial hair so I could shape what he had and add more where needed to accurately reflect the era.

This is where a current selfie, obtained beforehand, from the shoulders up, becomes essential to my process. I use it as a reference to base my sketches and design any additional facial hair prosthetics. It also allows me to match the prosthetic hair precisely to the actor's natural hair color, ensuring a seamless and authentic look on camera.

Being familiar with how to utilize the actor's selfie and transform it into a blueprint is a game-changer! Here are some tips that will help you begin your journey by analyzing characters.

## Actor's Selfie

☐ Request real-time selfies beforehand in good lighting from three angles: front, left profile, and right profile. These will help you assess facial structure and tailor your makeup approach.

☐ You can print an 8x10 color photo (shoulders up). This is what I do for each actor.

☐ Place the photo in a clear 8x10 plastic insert and store it in a three-ring binder.

☐ Sketch directly on the plastic insert with a reusable marker as you design the character.

☐ Use the photo for reshaping the hairline, restructuring facial features, and any special effects.

☐ Once completed, take a photo for future mobile use.

☐ On set, the 8x10 photo is what you'll focus on. Tape it up for reference during application.

☐ After filming, archive all character design sketches and notes taken during filming for possible reshoots. Your updated notes will allow you to recreate a scene with perfect continuity.

## Connecting With the Actors

Once the pre-production meeting is over and I have approval from the executive producer, I'll contact each actor and introduce myself. The first thing I explain to a female actor is why they shouldn't wax their face, get a facial, change skincare products, undergo a chemical peel or laser treatment, or use a tanning booth. These procedures can have unpredictable effects on the skin. Since the skin is a living organ, any damage can take weeks to heal, and that could mean the actor is out of a job.

When I first contact the female and male actors, I make it clear that they should not wear any jewelry, piercings, or makeup. If they arrive on set wearing makeup, it must be removed, and that takes time; time that isn't accounted for on the call sheet.

If the actor has a tattoo, I ask them to send me a photo, and I will make a note of it and consult with the costume designer to determine whether the tattoo will be visible or covered by the wardrobe.

Another important matter is to remind the actors not to wear colored or clear nail polish, because it will reflect on the camera. This includes no polish for scenes if the actor is wearing open-toe shoes or will be barefoot. Remember to tell them, or you will be removing it, and if you haven't designated time for this, then you will lose out on time with the next actor. I do include a bottle of nail polish remover in my kit, as there is always someone who forgets. I'll hand them a paper towel and the bottle of nail polish remover and tell them to go outside and remove it themselves.

## FEMALE ACTORS

Below is an actual letter I sent to a female actor.

*Hi Carol,*

*Nice to meet you virtually! Lol. I'll be your hair and makeup person for the upcoming documentary. Could you please send me a selfie, in good lighting, from your shoulders up, and email it to me? If you have any tattoos, please take a picture of them and send them along to me, also. Much appreciated!*

*A few things to go over before I see you on the day of filming.*

**Please do not wash your hair on the day of filming. It's okay to wash it the day before, but don't braid, pin it up, or apply any hair products.*

*On the day of filming, please arrive wearing no jewelry or makeup. Do not apply foundation, powders, or any other type of cosmetic on your face, not even mascara. The cameras are sensitive, and we use special makeup for this. Please do wear an unscented moisturizer, which is very important. Also, hold off on facial waxing, facial services, new cosmetics, facial laser, or new facial skin products until after filming. It's a precaution to make sure you have no skin issues that could possibly affect the outcome of the makeup or filming.*

*Thanks, and see you soon!*

*Rhonda Cummings*

*Rc Makeup Artist-HMU Director*

## MALE ACTORS

If a male actor will be sporting any facial hair, I have him stop shaving completely until he sees me. It's easier for me if the actor grows his facial hair out completely. On the day of filming, I will reshape it to match the approved beard, mustache, and/or sideburn design. If more hair is needed for the face, I will apply crepe hair to the existing facial hair, then reshape it as the period of the film dictates. I also use crepe hair to fill in sparse areas on the actor's head. All crepe hair is made and prepared in the pre-production phase.

If the character is to be clean-shaven, I inform the actor not to shave the morning of filming, but to shave the evening before. I ask him to shave before bed, not twenty-four hours before he's due on set, because you will have some regrowth, and you don't want to deal with it. This is the most difficult issue I have with male actors who must be clean-shaven. I do carry several electric shavers, but to get that close, especially with high-resolution cameras, I would have to use a straight-edge blade. It's too risky to shave within hours of filming, especially if the actor nicks his skin and it bleeds. Be adamant about the shaving, or you'll regret it. You cannot hide a beard!

Here is a letter I sent to a male actor whom I had the pleasure of working with on a prior film:

*Hi Steven,*

*I'm looking forward to working with you again on the upcoming documentary. My colleague, first assistant Aleah, and I will be handling your hair and makeup while on set. Please take a selfie, shoulders up, and forward it to me. The character you'll be portraying calls for you to be sporting an 1860s mustache and sideburns. You can stop shaving until I see you. I most likely will be adding some facial hair and will inform you once I get your headshots and collaborate with the producer on your exact look. I don't remember you having any allergies, correct? Also, send me updates on your tattoos and any new ones.*

*You'll be in my chair for at least two hours, or more, depending on how many of your tattoos will be exposed, and I won't know for sure until I speak with wardrobe about your costume. There are a few more things I need to go over with you prior to filming. Some might not pertain to you, but I must notify everyone.*

**No makeup at all, please. You can apply unscented moisturizer.*

**No nail polishes—not even clear.*

**No body piercings allowed that will be shown on camera.*

**No jewelry, necklaces, or rings, as there are no safes on set.*

**No perfumes, aftershave lotions, or scented creams due to others having possible allergies.*

*The weather forecasts rain, so bring a raincoat and a head protector.*

*If you have any questions, you know you can contact me directly. See you soon!*

*Rhonda*

*Rc Makeup Artist-HMU Director*

## 4 FINAL KEY THOUGHTS

- ☐ Analyze the manuscript to design the character's makeup effectively.
- ☐ Work closely with the costume designer to ensure collaboration and cohesive designs.
- ☐ Be aware of any allergies to the actors and the film crew.
- ☐ Keep detailed records, including photos, and all products used on each actor.

11:59:57:06
ROLL 1/48
SCENE GHOST WALK
TAKE 3
PROD HTH WOMAN OF OLD MANSE

CHAPTER 5

# During Production

Throughout my career, I've had incredible opportunities to work with actors and film crews from all over the United States, and even from different countries. Each professional brought their own unique skills and perspective to the filmmaking process, and it's truly fascinating to see all our contributions come together to create something magical on the big screen.

By the time we've reached day one of filming, I'll have already been introduced to several of the film crew during our pre-production meetings. These meetings can take place in a variety of ways. For the last twelve years, Zoom has been a lifesaver, as everyone can join in at the same time! Five years prior to that, in 2004, Facebook was launched, and it was good for conference calls, but Zoom changed everything for me. Prior to that, meetings were always held in person, and I had to travel in my car to them.

Regardless of how the film crew first connects, these early days of interactions are crucial. It allows us to start building relationships and a sense of camaraderie before we set foot on the film set. It's in these moments that I begin to understand the dynamics of everyone's role and get a feel for the creative energy that will drive the project forward.

## The Film Crew and Their Responsibilities

On the left is Cinematographer Allie Humenuk, filming an 1840s historical reenactment parade we did in Lexington, Massachusetts. On the right is Cinematographer Keith Walker and Rhonda during the filming of a Frederick Douglass documentary in the summer of 2023 in Washington, D.C.

Understanding a film crew and their roles can be overwhelming, but it's to your advantage to know the specific responsibilities of each crew member on set.

You will witness this group of highly skilled professionals come together, guided by a film production company and directed by the executive producer, to bring a manuscript to life on screen. Each member plays a vital role in turning the written vision into a visual masterpiece. From the director shaping the narrative and guiding performances to the cinematographer capturing stunning visuals, to the sound recordist ensuring crystal-clear audio, to the gaffer ensuring the lighting ambiance is on target. Everyone works in harmony to create the final product.

Left, Danielle Bryant, DP, and Actor Anthony Gaudette are deep in the woods filming *Cling*, a thriller mystery. On the right, Director Jon Heutmaker and Danielle set up for another scene.

As part of the film crew, I contribute my own expertise to this collaborative process in a challenging environment, where each person's talent and dedication help transform ideas into reality. I've had the privilege of working with some truly exceptional people during my career. Knowing what their jobs entail and how they relate to mine has been incredibly helpful. The dedication, skill, and teamwork these individuals demonstrated have made a significant impact on every project we've collaborated on. Each of them brings unique talents that elevate the quality of our work. I'm always inspired by their commitment to excellence and by how they contribute to creating a seamless, successful production.

Understanding a film crew and what they do is overwhelming, but it's to your advantage to know this talented group!

Left to right: Aleah Harris (HMU), Jenny Alexandra (producer), James Mylord (actor), Anne Tubiolo (producer), Rhonda Cummings (HMU director), and Kevin Bryant (actor) on set of filming of the Frederick Douglass documentary in Washington, D.C.

## ACTOR

An actor is a performer who portrays a character in film, theater, television, or other media.

- ☐ Uses their voice, movement, expression, and emotions to bring the manuscript to life

## EXECUTIVE PRODUCER

The executive producer, known as the EP, can be likened to a ship's captain. A vessel relies on its captain for navigation; a film depends on its EP for direction.

- ☐ Oversees the development of the manuscript into a full-fledged film project
- ☐ Manages the production from concept to final on-screen product
- ☐ Handles logistical and business aspects of the film
- ☐ May delegate tasks to assistant producers

## ASSISTANT PRODUCER

The executive producer has one or more assistants, often called assistant producers. The assistant producer assigned to you will be your primary contact on set.

- ☐ Prepares and distributes the daily call sheet to each crew member
- ☐ Acts as the main on-set contact for clear communication and quick problem-solving
- ☐ Keeps the team updated throughout filming to anticipate and resolve issues
- ☐ Maintains workflow and serves as liaison with the executive producer
- ☐ Alerts the crew to breaks and meals to ensure the filming stays on schedule
- ☐ Ensures smooth production through strong organization and communication

## EXECUTIVE DIRECTOR

The position of the executive director, known as the ED, holds a pivotal role in the filmmaking process that goes beyond storytelling and scene guidance.

- ☐ May assist in casting of actors and crew members
- ☐ Collaborates with the EP from early development to align with financial goals
- ☐ Coordinates production elements to effectively translate the creative vision to the screen
- ☐ Leads on set, guiding actors, and making creative decisions to uphold the film's vision
- ☐ Works closely with all departments for visual and narrative cohesion
- ☐ Oversees post-production and planning of marketing efforts

## PRODUCTION DESIGNER

A production designer is a creative visionary responsible for defining the film's overall look and feel.

- ☐ Translates the manuscript into a cohesive and visual narrative
- ☐ Establishes the film's visual style through color palettes, textures, and architecture
- ☐ Begins collaboration in pre-production with the EP, ED, and cinematographer
- ☐ Oversees set construction to accurately reflect the time period, location, and emotional tone
- ☐ Partners with the set decorator to enhance authenticity with props and décor
- ☐ Scouts locations or works with the location manager to secure filming sites

## DIRECTOR OF PHOTOGRAPHY (CINEMATOGRAPHER)

Also known as the DP, responsible for bringing a film's visual essence to fruition through cinematography.

- ☐ Shares lighting and camera specs with the MUA for tailored makeup techniques
- ☐ Ensures MUA looks are consistent and flattering under all lighting conditions and completes joint camera/makeup tests
- ☐ Immediately addresses any issues spotted during tests

## DIRECTOR OF LIGHTING (GAFFER)

The director of lighting, known as the gaffer, diligently adjusts lights and assures us the set is ready for action.

- ☐ Strategically places light to enhance scenes and highlight the actor's face

□ Works with the key MUA to ensure optimal lighting for makeup

## SOUND RECORDIST

The technical term for the person in charge of sound is a sound recordist. Often works on the same actor simultaneously with the MUA to adjust or place mics.

□ Selects and places microphones for all actors

□ Captures every word, breath, and nuance for maximum impact

## DIRECTOR OF MAKEUP (MUA DIRECTOR)

The role of the director of makeup is a pivotal position within the film production team and an honor. They work closely with the EP and the costume designer throughout the entire film.

□ Responsible for researching the films period

□ Conceptualizes each character's look based on time period, fashion, and cultural nuances

□ Prepares designs for the EP and costume designer in pre-production for approval

□ Adheres strictly to approved makeup designs; any alterations require the EP's sign-off

## KEY MAKEUP ARTIST (KEY MUA)

The role of a key MUA often extends beyond applying makeup. This role requires strong communication and coordination skills.

□ May also serve as the makeup director when working solo

□ Attends meetings to align on expectations and design continuity

□ Applies and maintains approved makeup designs for lead cast members

- ☐ Coordinates with the costume designer on makeup for the film's overall look
- ☐ Acts as both a hands-on artist and liaison to the makeup director on set

## PROFESSIONAL MAKEUP ARTIST (PROFESSIONAL MUA)

Being a professional MUA signifies an ascent up the career ladder. This achievement is typically attained through apprenticeship programs or extended periods of assisting experienced MUAs.

- ☐ Responsible for executing makeup looks assigned by the key or makeup director
- ☐ Shows strong attention to detail and strict adherence to guidelines
- ☐ Trusted with the final design looks, reflecting proficiency and reliability
- ☐ Works under the key MUA, which sharpens technical skills and builds resilience

## SPECIAL EFFECTS MAKEUP (SFX MUA)

A special effects makeup artist, also known as an SFX MUA, creates transformative, often dramatic, visual effects on actors' faces and bodies for film, television, theater, and other productions.

- ☐ Utilizes prosthetics, latex, silicone, or wax to create visuals that support the story
- ☐ Designs looks for aging, injuries, fantasy creatures, and realistic wounds
- ☐ Engages in sculpting, molding, painting, and applying prosthetics
- ☐ Ensures the durability of effects under various lighting conditions and long hours

☐ Maintains continuity, on-set adjustments, and safely removes prosthetics

## ASSISTANT MAKEUP ARTIST (ASSISTANT MUA)

An assistant MUA is responsible for supporting the key MUA in executing the makeup design.

☐ Shows strong attention to detail and strict adherence to guidelines

☐ Trusted with final looks, reflecting proficiency and reliability

☐ Utilizes problem-solving abilities in a fast-paced, high-pressure environment

☐ Fosters growth, creativity, and practical contribution to the MUA team

Understand that breaking into the film industry as an assistant makeup artist takes time and resilience. Stay adaptable and open to opportunities by applying for entry-level positions, such as collaborating with film students and independent filmmakers, to gain practical experience on film sets. Be willing to start with small, independent projects to build your credibility.

Network aggressively and attend industry events, film festivals, and workshops to meet professionals. Don't forget to keep in touch with classmates, instructors, and contacts made during internships, as you never know where your next subcontracting job will come from. Everyone loves to recommend a talented and reliable worker!

Don't forget to market yourself effectively with an online presence, including a professional-looking website and social media platforms. I love using social media on set to share what is happening behind the scenes in real time.

## DIRECTOR OF HAIR AND MAKEUP

In many instances, the key makeup artist and the key hairdresser merge into one skilled professional, commonly known as the director of hair and makeup (HMU).

This job encompasses everything the makeup director is responsible for, including hair and wig needs.

- ☐ Create hair and makeup charts for characters that align with the film's time period
- ☐ Has a deep understanding of period-specific hairstyles, makeup, and experience in wig application and styling

I enjoy serving as the director of HMU on a film project. As a seasoned cosmetologist with forty years of experience, I believe I have the perfect trifecta by being a makeup artist, hairdresser, and wig stylist. This has become my niche. Having the ability to integrate these three services seamlessly has positioned me as an asset to any production that is both non-union and with the permission of a union, to partake in production. Whether your goal is to be the director of HMU on a film or start with an internship, I encourage you to choose your educational journey wisely and investigate cosmetology schools.

## COSTUME DESIGNER

The costume designer works closely with the MUA throughout production. Costume designers play a vital role in shaping the film's visual narrative, enhancing the storytelling, and bringing the characters to life.

- ☐ Manages costume budgets, vendors, and timelines to stay on schedule
- ☐ Designs historically era-appropriate costumes based on a manuscript

- ☐ Oversees creation, sourcing, and alteration of costumes
- ☐ Adjusts designs with input from the director, producer, and actors
- ☐ Maintains direct communication with the MUA throughout production

## WRANGLER

If you see a category on the call sheet titled "wrangler," you might ask, "What is this person responsible for?" Their main goal is to manage and coordinate the handling of specific elements. The various types of wranglers include:

### CROWD WRANGLER

- ☐ Handle large groups of people for crowd scenes

### ANIMAL WRANGLER

- ☐ Trains animals to perform in scenes and stunts
- ☐ Cares for animals and ensures their safety on set

### CHILD WRANGLER

- ☐ Supervises young actors to keep them focused and avoid boredom
- ☐ Oversees schoolwork and educational activities as needed

### VEHICLE WRANGLER

- ☐ Sources and manages vehicles used in production
- ☐ Maintains the condition of vehicles and prepares for filming

## WEAPONS MASTER VS. ARMORER

I found this category very interesting when I was first learning how to read a call sheet. Both positions serve as liaisons among the producer, director, and actors on a film set. The difference is:

### WEAPONS MASTER

- ☐ Oversees all weapons on set (guns, knives, swords, etc.)
- ☐ Ensures safety, training, script accuracy, and legal compliance
- ☐ Coordinates with the film crew
- ☐ May supervise armorers

### ARMORER

- ☐ Specializes in firearms
- ☐ Handles the safety and maintenance of firearms
- ☐ Provides firearm training to actors
- ☐ Often works under the weapons master on larger sets

# Understanding a Call Sheet

The call sheet is a crucial document that you'll receive daily, which serves as the central hub for communication. It ensures the film crew is well-informed and aligned with the day's schedule. It provides a wealth of information, including call times for crew and actors, scene locations, contact information for key personnel, the weather forecast, designated parking, nearby hospitals, potential hazards at shooting locations, and more.

Furthermore, the call sheet serves as an official record of attendance and participation for everyone involved in a production. It documents call times, meal breaks, wrap times, and hours worked for everyone, ensuring fair compensation and compliance with labor agreements. It maintains compliance with labor regulations by outlining required rest periods and maximum working hours for actors and crew. The call sheet may be used for legal and insurance purposes as it records crucial details of the filming process.

It is advisable to search online for free film call sheets to familiarize yourself with the various types, styles, and formats available. Gaining this knowledge can be incredibly helpful. Makeup artists and hairdressers are usually listed on the call sheet under the arts department.

I have developed a bedtime ritual: I never go to sleep without reading the call sheet for the next day. The first thing I do in the morning is check my emails and text messages for last-minute changes. Once any changes are noted, I will print myself a copy of the whole call sheet.

As I've mentioned previously, the call sheet dictates the day's schedule and helps you with figuring out locations for the "home base" and "on location" shoots. Be aware of the weather. If you are filming outdoors, you need to dress according to the weather forecast. Production will prepare a covered, dry area adjacent to the filming location. This is where you'll apply makeup touch-ups.

Each season brings its own set of weather challenges, and as an MUA, you'll need to learn how to adapt and come up with real-time solutions. In the summer, you'll have to deal with sweating; in the winter, it might be windburn and the risk of frostbite. Fall usually offers cooler but manageable weather, while spring often brings rain and dampness. The weather for each day will dictate how you dress, what you pack in your kit, and which tools you'll need to use.

When it's raining or snowing, you'll need to adjust your makeup approach. Make sure all your waterproof products are ready in your master kit. Keep everything stored in waterproof cases or plastic Ziploc bags to protect your supplies. Waterproof clothing and boots are essential, as you don't want to be cold and wet on set. Always keep an extra set of clothing in your personal bag, just in case.

If you're filming indoors, be prepared for different kinds of challenges. Lighting will be at the top of this list. Proper communication here can make a big difference in how your work appears on camera.

## Slang Words

Be aware of some crazy words you'll hear on set. I remember trying to find the ladies' bathroom, and I was told the "honey wagon" room was in the next building. I told them I didn't want to go to the "honey wagon" room location; I just needed to use the ladies' room. They laughed at me and said, "That's what we call the bathrooms!"

Here are some words you might see used on a call sheet or verbalized while on set.

- ☐ **Honey wagon**: Slang for the bathroom area on set
- ☐ **Side**: A small handout with last-minute details about the day's shoot
- ☐ **Split day**: Part of the work is filmed in the a.m. and the rest in the p.m.
- ☐ **Call time**: When you are expected to arrive on set
- ☐ **Holding**: A designated area for actors to wait before filming
- ☐ **Lock it up**: A call to quiet down as filming is about to begin
- ☐ **Wrap**: The end of filming is completed for the day

You'll feel like a pro on set just knowing the above slang words.

## Location Set Up and Etiquette

There are a few things I always go over with my team before we arrive on set. To start, punctuality is vital from the time of arrival to the last scene. This keeps the production schedule on time. My team always meets thirty minutes before the scheduled arrival time that's been assigned on the call sheet. This gives us time to finish our coffees, collect our thoughts, and gives me time to prepare them for the day and address any overnight changes. I will reiterate to each team member to maintain complete confidentiality and the privacy of the actors and film crew. This includes no social media postings unless approved by production. If a problem arises while filming, my team communicates with me directly, and I will rectify the situation or call the first assistant producer if necessary.

Upon arrival at the film location, you will be given a piece of paper with the words "parking pass" and place it inside your car on the front window, demonstrating that you have permission to park with the film crew, and an identification badge will be assigned to you that must always be worn while on set.

I suggest that you do not unpack your makeup cases until you are directed to the unloading area and parking area. It brings back memories of a film project that Rozy D and I worked on. The film was to take place inside a breathtaking 1800s mansion. It continues to be one of my favorite filming jobs.

On the first day of the filming, Rozy and I drove to the location noted on the call sheet. We pulled right up to the front door of a beautiful mansion and started unloading my car. Once everything was out, I got back into the car and parked to the right of the building. Then I walked back to the front door and waited for the film crew to arrive and let us in. Just a few minutes later, a white van pulled up in front of us. A young man stepped out and said, "This isn't the mansion you're filming in; this was actually the servants' quarters back in the 1800s."

"Follow me," he added. You guessed it, I had to get the car and load everything up again. We followed him down a long driveway lined with towering pine trees on both sides until we finally reached the real mansion. What a lesson I learned that day!

## ARRIVAL

Upon arrival at the film set, I'll go to the area that is assigned to my team for the day. If I did my pre-production job correctly, I've let the executive producer know that I must be located as close as possible to the costume department with as much natural lighting as possible, which means windows, please and thank you. You want as much natural light as possible, and daylight is equivalent to a 600-watt light bulb. Look for plug outlets for your electric tools. I never set up near fire exits, entry doors, and bathrooms (too busy an area).

Once my team has acclimated to our designated workspace for that day, our first task is to pinpoint the location of the costume department. After we've identified the costume department's whereabouts, I immediately shift my attention to the tedious task of setting up our base of operations, ensuring that our workspace is not only functional but also conducive to productivity and creativity.

## CAMERA MUA CHECK

Here, attention to detail is paramount. As I have discussed previously, I carefully assess how the makeup translates on camera, ensuring it complements the character's portrayal and enhances the overall visual narrative.

As the makeup application progresses and the first actor is ready for their camera check, I transition to the set's filming area to observe the initial checks. One of my primary responsibilities involves working hand-in-hand with the gaffer and the director of cinematography to execute the camera makeup test. This crucial step not only ensures that the actors look their best on camera but also allows for adjustments to be made if necessary for the gaffer, guaranteeing a polished final product. This collaborative effort ensures that the visual elements will align with the vision of the film project.

## VIDEO VILLAGE CAMERA

The video village is my go-to spot on set once filming begins. This designated area is essentially the nerve center for viewing live filming. It's where key members of the creative team gather to monitor the action on screen in real time. It's also a collaborative hub where you can confer with the executive director and costume designer to ensure everything works together seamlessly. You and other crew members will look for anything out of place on the actors and zero in on any sign of shine on the face. I always let each actor know where I'll be located during filming, and if they feel sweaty, cold, or need help, they can just raise their hand towards me, and I'll be right over.

In short, my presence at Video Village is as much about maintaining creative quality as it is about problem-solving in real time. It's not just about seeing the work; it's about ensuring that every detail contributes to the storytelling exactly as intended.

## FILMING STUDIO

A filming studio is a physical space that provides the necessary infrastructure for film production. One specific type of studio with which I am well acquainted is the green screen studio. My involvement in this field involves extensive research, particularly since 90 percent of my work within this environment pertains to documentaries, demanding meticulous attention to historical accuracy.

## GREEN SCREEN STUDIO

Over the past twelve years, I've had the privilege of working in many different green screen studios. These filming studios encompass various components, such as soundstages, backlots, equipment services, post-production facilities, equipment rentals, wardrobe and costume departments, hair and makeup facilities, catering rooms, and designated filming areas.

When working in a green screen studio, it's crucial to understand how the green backdrop can impact makeup. Green often reflects onto the skin, casting an ashy or unnatural tone. To prevent this, you should always do a camera makeup test check after the foundation has been applied and again before filming begins. This allows you to identify and adjust any potential issues caused by the green screen lighting.

Stepping into a green screen studio is like walking into a different world. The controlled lighting, seamless green walls, ceilings, and even the floors can be covered in green to create a unique atmosphere. I learned this lesson the hard way. I had no idea what to expect the first time I worked in this type of environment. As I stepped into the area to conduct my camera makeup pre-check, I suddenly heard a man yell in a very deep voice, "Stop, do not take another step with your shoes on!"

My heart nearly stopped as I looked down and saw that my sneakers had left a visible mark on the flooring. Thankfully, the marks didn't show during filming, but it was a mistake I'll never forget.

For me, this environment demands heightened attention to detail. Adjusting makeup to balance the green color effect under studio lighting requires collaboration with the gaffer and a keen eye for color correction on my behalf. Every color and detail matters, especially when the final product relies on digital backgrounds and effects. These challenges are part of what makes working in a green screen studio so exciting. It's a space where creativity meets precision, and every detail contributes to the magic of filmmaking.

## CRAFT SERVICE AND CATERING SERVICES

I cannot stress enough the importance of knowing where the food services are located. It's essential to distinguish the difference between craft services and catering services, especially considering the potential for long hours on set, which typically span ten to twelve hours.

Craft services are mobile and will be accompanying the film crew to various locations throughout the day. This ensures that all crew members have access to water and snacks, even when away from the main base camp. On the other hand, catering services are typically stationed at the home base camp or the on-location site for the day. In most cases, the hair, makeup, and costume departments are given priority for lunch and dinner before the cast and crew break. If I have a team on set, I make it a priority to ensure that everyone is aware of and utilizes these food services to maintain energy levels throughout the demanding shooting schedule.

## ACTOR'S GREEN ROOM

The green room is a backstage haven where actors can relax, prepare, and regroup before stepping in front of the camera. It serves as a small sanctuary away from the controlled chaos of the set, providing a space where performers can recharge and focus. Beyond preparation, it's a place to decompress between takes. Filming can be grueling, with long hours under bright lights and intense focus.

The actors use this room for various purposes. It's common to see someone sitting quietly in a corner, rehearsing their lines under their breath, or pacing back and forth while working through an intense monologue. Others might take the opportunity to meditate, stretch, or mentally prepare for a demanding scene. It's also a space for camaraderie, where the actors provide moral support to one another before stepping into the spotlight.

The green room is also a hub for collaboration, and I often find myself there doing last-minute touch-ups. The director or producer might pop in to discuss last-minute changes to a scene, or the costume designer may swing by to make quick adjustments. The green room becomes a dynamic space where everyone works together to keep the production running smoothly, all while maintaining a calm and supportive environment for the actors.

# Interacting with the Costume Designer

Maintaining effective communication with the costume designer is essential, not just during pre-production but throughout the entire filming process. This ongoing dialogue allows us to address any necessary adjustments or modifications, ensuring visual coherence across the board. The way you communicate on set will depend on the production's scale, with communication directed either through the crew or via a walkie-talkie provided for direct contact with senior members.

Once we've acclimated to our designated workspace for that day, our first task is to pinpoint the location of the costume department. After we've identified the costume department's whereabouts, I immediately shift my attention to the tedious task of setting up our base of operations, ensuring that our workspace is not only functional but also conducive to productivity and creativity.

It's crucial to remember one golden rule: once filming starts, never handle the actors' costumes. If the costume designer is absent but their expertise is required to fix a costume issue, refrain from taking matters into your own hands, particularly on union film sets. Instead, I immediately seek assistance from the first assistant in costume, who is often nearby and readily available to help. Your primary focus is on makeup, and the last thing you want to risk is staining costumes with makeup residue. The same principle applies to hair: if you need to move the actor's hair to apply makeup, always defer to the hair department. While it may seem trivial, adhering to this protocol ensures professionalism and avoids any potential mishaps.

## Just a Reminder

A few last things I want to mention. I always maintain order and cleanliness, no matter where I am or where my crew is set up. One rule that never changes: if I make trash, I take it with me on the way out! All phones must be completely silenced and cannot make any noise once filming starts. Sometimes we are told to shut all phones off completely, as they may interfere with equipment.

Another important thing to remember is that if you are also in charge of doing hair, do not have hairspray near the cameras. If I do need to use any hair products, they will be in liquid form with a spray pump. When I do use hair sprays, I will not spray it in the filming area. I'll go back to the makeup room or take a walk outside in the hallway so as not to have these particles floating near production. These types of products have very high glosses when they dry. You do not want this, as it will reflect onto the camera. I notify all actors beforehand not to apply any hair products at their last washing before they see me on set.

## Post-Production

One of the key post-production responsibilities I take seriously, and one you'll want to prioritize too, is guiding actors in returning their costumes to wardrobe. Once they've done that, they'll come to you for help removing their makeup, facial prosthetics, or facial hair. It's your job to make sure the actors leave the film set looking just like they did when they arrived.

Be thorough and efficient during the post-production stage. It may seem like a small task, but it plays a major role in wrapping the day smoothly and professionally. The way you handle this process reflects your commitment to the bigger picture. Always aim for seamless collaboration with the costume designer. Clear communication and mutual respect between departments are essential. When you work in harmony, you elevate the entire production, and that's the kind of MUA every film set needs.

## 5 FINAL KEY THOUGHTS

Upon arrival, I'll go to the area that is assigned to us for the day. If I did my pre-production job correctly, I've let the executive producer who hired me know that I must be located as close as possible to the costume department and need as much natural lighting as possible, which means windows, please and thank you. You want as much natural lighting as possible, as daylight is 600-watts. Look for windows and plug outlets. I never set up near fire exits, entry doors, and bathrooms (too busy of an area—unless the bathroom is my homebase).

- ☐ **Know the film crew** and understand the hierarchy and roles within the team.
- ☐ **Understand a call sheet**, how to read call times, scene breakdowns, and special notes.
- ☐ **Set up efficiently** and always follow proper **on-set etiquette.**
- ☐ **Collaborate with the costume designer** to ensure cohesive character looks.
- ☐ **Be available for reshoots** and **postproduction enhancements** when necessary.

Producer, director, and writer, Jonathan Heutmaker, on set with Rhonda

# CHAPTER 6

# Basic Special Effects

I can't help but smile whenever a manuscript calls for special effects makeup (SFX MU), especially when it involves aging an actor, creating facial hair, or achieving a specific period look for a documentary film. As I share some first-hand experiences in this chapter, I'll provide insight into the basic tools and the fundamental techniques that I've come to rely on when creating impactful designs.

Becoming truly skilled in SFX MU requires more than just creativity; it takes serious technical training. Having a working knowledge of how to create a realistic bruise, scrape, or basic cut is essential because it makes you an asset to any production. You will need to understand how injuries progress over time, how aging changes the skin's texture and tone, and how lighting will dramatically affect the final look of your work.

Performing basic special effects doesn't make you a specialist in SFX MUA, not by any means! Earning that title requires intense, specialized training. It's an incredibly rewarding path, but it demands real commitment, and it all starts with mastering the fundamentals. If a film requires more advanced SFX MU than what you can perform, then it's your responsibility to communicate that clearly to the executive producer and secure approval to bring an additional SFX MUA onto your team.

# Developing SFX MU Designs

When I'm developing SFX MU designs, my process is both meticulous and creative. It's built around three key steps that feel like second nature to me, and if you're looking to succeed in this field, I recommend you make them part of your process too:

**1. Start with the Manuscript**

I can't stress enough that the manuscript is everything. I often call it my Bible, as it guides me through the entire creative journey. The manuscript will give you every detail you need: the character's backstory, the timeline, and the setting. All of this helps ensure your designs align with the story. Don't skip this step!

**2. Establish a Vision**

Before I create a single look, I make sure I fully understand the executive producer and director's visions. This is where I present my SFX-MU portfolio books. They're an invaluable resource during the first pre-production meeting. Once I've received clarity, I'll move on to collaborate with the costume designer, then with the actor.

**3. Keep Detailed Records**

Documentation is non-negotiable, and everyone who works with me will testify to that. I take numerous photos, both color and black-and-white, to capture the progression of each look. All information will go into a white three-ring binder with detailed records of every product, formula, technique, and in the exact order it was applied. Documenting the actual time spent with each actor is a must for future retakes of a scene.

# SFX MU Basic Essentials Kit

## CREAM COLOR WHEELS

When you look inside my SFX MU kit, you'll quickly notice that it stands apart from all my other kits. I've tailored it specifically to meet the diverse needs of creating realistic special effects for stage, film, and special events. My kit contains six cream-colored wheels with a five-color palette. With these six wheels, customizing any color is possible.

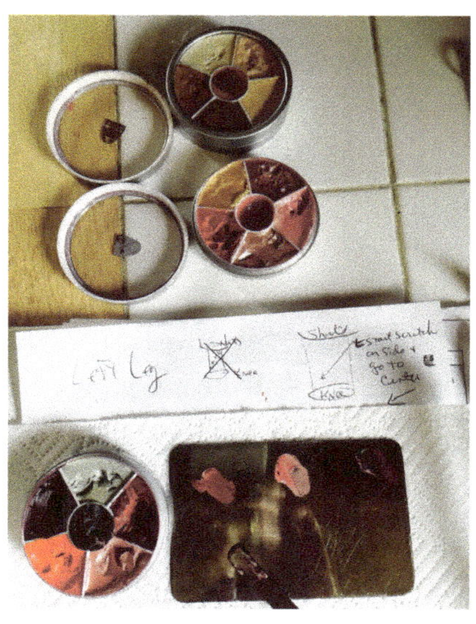

Additionally, I have cream-colored wheels in all black and all white. I use these wheels for lighting or darkening a customized color. This is where I utilize my one-to-ten mixing method to get the exact color I need. Know your color theory, or you'll be lugging cases and cases of individual colors in cream, powder, and liquid form!

## PALETTE KNIFE AND SPATULA

My palette knives and spatulas are two tools I can't work without. On any given day, I carry at least six of each with me. My makeup assistant will ensure they're always clean, sanitized, and ready to be used. Whether I'm mixing creams, applying wax or gelatin onto the skin, or even scratching powdered colors from a tin, these tools make my work seamless.

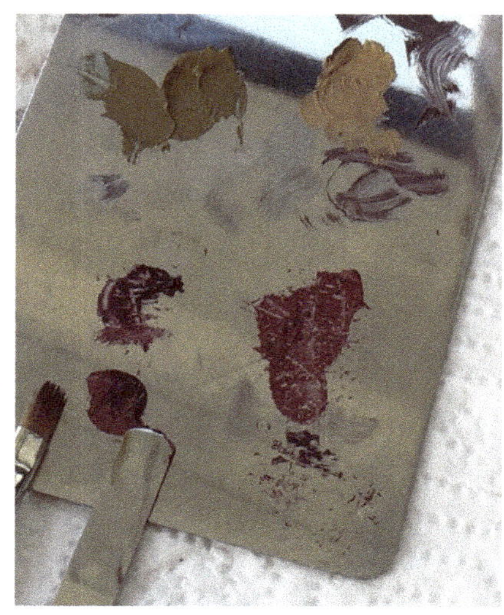

There's something about the feel and versatility of metal ones that I absolutely love. I use these tools for so many tasks. One thing I love is how the metal can be cold to the touch, which can be incredibly useful. And when I need warmth, I just place a hot, wet hand towel underneath, transforming the palette into a heated surface that softens creams effortlessly.

## Special Effects Makeup Brushes

I have a diverse array of synthetic special effects makeup brushes that are indispensable tools to my craft. The choice between brushes is determined by what type of SFX MU design I'll be applying to the actor.

I typically carry a minimum of seventy-five makeup brushes per day on set when dealing with a cast of four actors to ensure I am well-equipped for any scenario. Three-quarters of these brushes are typically synthetic, as I use cream-based makeup far more than water-based makeup for these types of applications.

Additionally, synthetic brushes become essential when I have an actor who is allergic to animal hair. I once encountered an actor who had a sensitivity, not a true allergy; however, I treated it as if it were a true allergy. In this case, I prepared a special actor's kit that was free of animal hair products and applied his makeup in a separate room to accommodate his needs.

## SPONGES

### BLACK AND ORANGE STIPPLE BLOCK SPONGES

The black stipple block sponge is an incredibly versatile tool. Made of firm plastic, it features an open-weave design with irregular patterns running throughout. It comes in various thicknesses and widths, making it ideal for creating realistic textures on the skin, such as scrapes, cuts, and even aging effects. I especially love using it for applying techniques to create large areas of bruising on the body.

I buy large blocks of this sponge and then cut individual pieces to suit the specific needs of each project. For detailed work, I often trim the blocks down to as small as a half inch by half inch. This allows me to apply textures with precision and create intricate effects. Customizing the sponges in this way ensures that I can achieve exactly the results I'm aiming for, whether the work is subtle or dramatic. It's all about adapting tools to the project's scale and requirements, and this sponge never lets me down!

## ORANGE RUBBER STIPPLE BLOCK SPONGE

The orange rubber stipple block sponge is a coarsely textured, square-shaped sponge that is indispensable for certain SFX MU looks. Its rough texture allows me to create highly textured looks while still blending seamlessly. These sponges are available in natural latex, synthetic, and polyurethane, each offering slightly different results.

I particularly love using this sponge for aging techniques, as it's perfect for creating realistic wrinkles and adding depth to an aged appearance. It's also incredibly effective for enhancing the texture of a black eye, making the overall effect look more authentic. Additionally, I sometimes rely on this sponge when applying adhesives to large areas of skin. Its unique texture ensures even distribution of the adhesive without compromising the skin's natural appearance.

## RED RUBBER FLAT STIPPLE SPONGE

The red rubber flat stipple sponge is an absolute must-have in my SFX MU kit. This sponge is made from dense foam rubber. Its design makes it perfect for adding a textured finish that mimics the natural pores on the skin for a believable effect.

I rely on this sponge when working on bald capping or applying small appliances or prosthetics. Its dense structure allows me to blend edges to ensure the piece integrates naturally with the actor's skin. This sponge is also my first choice for creating realistic finishes on other areas of the body, such as the fine texture of scars, burns, or aged skin.

### BASIC WHITE MAKEUP SPONGE

Your basic white makeup sponge is not only used for applying foundation and blending makeup, but also for creating different textures. It comes in latex and non-latex. These days, you can find the basic white sponge in every color and size you can think of.

# Choosing the Correct Adhesive

In SFX MU, selecting the correct adhesive is crucial for achieving a secure and long-lasting application. Over time, I've learned that the best choice of adhesive depends on factors like skin type, environmental conditions, and the type of prosthetic or piece being applied. Additionally, there are specialized adhesives that are designed to better withstand sweat and moisture, ensuring durability in high-heat or high-performance environments. Each type has unique properties, allowing me to choose the best option for specific projects.

Prior to filming, I always ask the actor if they have any allergies or skin sensitivities and perform a pre-test on the inside of their forearm with the adhesive I'll be using. I will ask the actor to arrive thirty minutes before their scheduled call time for this pre-test.

Having the proper products and tools for removing the adhesive is just as important as the application itself. I spend the money and get the safest and gentlest adhesive removers so they don't cause terrible skin irritations to the actor. Always follow the manufacturer's directions. By taking these steps, I make sure the actor's skin remains healthy, irritation-free, and ready for the next scene.

## SPIRIT GUM ADHESIVE

Spirit gum adhesives come in several types, and each is designed to meet different needs for different applications. Traditionally, they are made from natural resin and are ideal for securing lightweight prosthetics, facial hair, and wigs.

☐ Matte spirit gum is a matte formulation that offers a non-shiny finish, making it perfect for camera work where reflections must be minimized.

☐ Clear spirit gum dries transparently, providing a seamless look, and is particularly useful for intricate or delicate applications.

☐ Water-based spirit gum is a gentler alternative, suitable for sensitive skin or short-term use, as it's easier to remove.

# Pros-Aide Adhesive

Pros-Aide adhesive is my go-to when applying prosthetics, especially heavier ones. As a professional-grade adhesive, its superior bonding strength and unique formulation make it indispensable in my work. One of its standout features is its water resistance, ensuring prosthetics stay securely in place even under challenging conditions like sweat, humidity, or exposure to water. Its long-lasting bond is dependable, and its reliability is crucial for successful applications.

I also prefer Pros-Aide adhesive because it's a water-based acrylic adhesive, making it safer for prolonged use on the skin. It's my top choice for actors with sensitive skin, as it's less likely to cause irritation compared to other adhesives. Knowing that it's both effective and gentle gives me peace of mind when working on extended filming days or demanding stage performances.

The removal of Pros-Aide adhesive requires care and preparation. If I don't properly prepare the skin before application, removal will become tricky. To address this, I always keep Pros-Aide adhesive remover on hand. It was more expensive but worth every penny! This product dissolves the adhesive safely and effectively, ensuring I can remove prosthetics without causing damage or discomfort to the actor's skin.

### LIQUID LATEX

Liquid latex is another one of my go-to SFX MU products because of its incredible versatility. I use it to create realistic wounds or build up textures directly on the skin. Whether I need to mimic burns, scars, aged skin, or other effects, liquid latex does the job. It's available in various colors. I can choose just one that matches the look I'm creating, or I can layer and paint over it for added realism. Liquid latex is made from either natural or synthetic rubber latex, making it flexible and durable enough to hold up under the demands of filming. It's a staple in my kit. It's perfect for creating lifelike injuries that are essential in action scenes.

For removal, I use warm soapy water, which makes the product peel right off. This is a big plus for both the actor and me after a long day on a set.

## Blood Wounds

When it comes to creating realistic bloody effects, understanding the timeline of the injury is essential. The amount of time that has passed since the injury occurred determines not only the color of the blood but also the appearance of surrounding bruises. Fresh injuries typically feature bright red blood, while older wounds develop darker, almost brown hues, with bruising starting to show in shades of purple, blue, and yellow.

To get the details correct, I'll go directly to my injury morgue portfolio books, especially if there are no visual references sent to me. These books are useful references with images of wounds and injuries at various stages. During the first pre-production meeting, I always present these pictures to the executive producer and director. It's crucial to have them choose a look or provide me with specific reference pictures because assuming what they want can lead to costly mistakes. Blood effects must be precise and match the scene's narrative and emotional tone.

## LIQUID BLOOD
Actor Anthoney Gaudette and Cinematographer Danielle Bryant.

On fresh injuries, I typically use liquid blood because the viscosity mimics fresh blood. The consistency is thinner, and it flows more easily. This is my go-to for creating cuts and wounds when filming in real time, as it makes the actor appear to be actively bleeding.

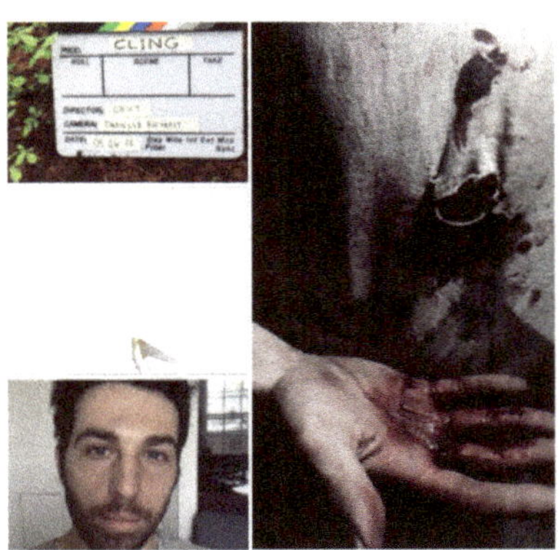

## THICKENED LIQUID BLOOD
Deep wound by Rhonda Cummings

One of the best things about using liquid blood is that it can be thickened if needed by adding cornstarch. It's so versatile that I've used it for both small cuts and large wounds. My SFX MU kit consists of numerous bottles of liquid blood in different shades. Most of the time, I customize colors by mixing and matching.

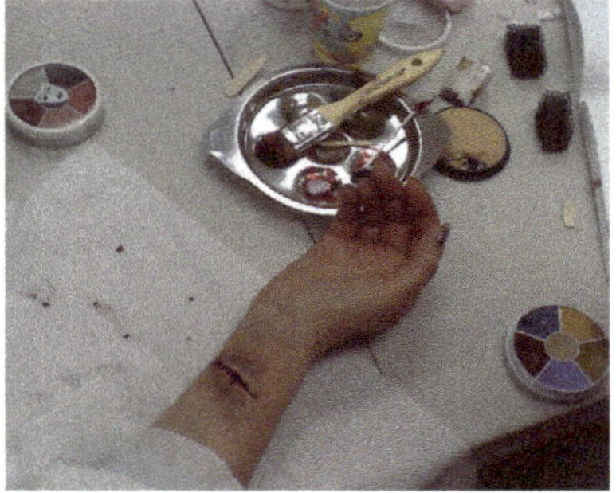

## BLOOD PASTE

Blood paste is one of my favorite tools for creating realistic injuries. Its thick, sticky consistency perfectly mimics coagulated or crusted blood, especially for older or more severe wounds. It's an essential product in my kit. For the above knee injury, I used cream-based products on a black stipple sponge to create scratches, then texturized with blood paste on a synthetic brush.

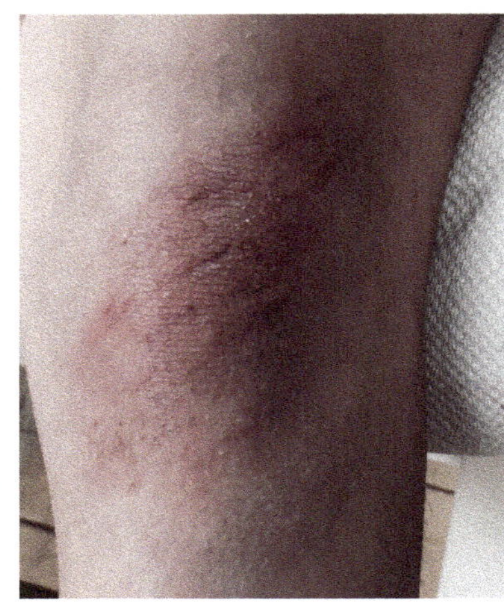

Injury created on an actor who played a character who fell off their bicycle.

## BLOOD CAPSULES

I use blood capsules when the scene calls for blood that needs to flow, come out of the mouth, or occur from a gunshot wound. The capsules are filled with non-toxic fluid made to be easily bitten into or burst on cue. They're perfect for adding that extra level of realism in scenarios like mouth wounds or injuries where blood is supposed to ooze or spill out dramatically. I've used these capsules several times for fight scenes.

## SCRAPES AND SCRATCHES

Designing scrapes and scratches is one of the easiest tasks for me. I start by putting dark colored cream makeup onto a black stipple sponge with a synthetic brush. I then apply it onto the skin in short, quick "on and off" motion to the injured area. The key to getting the look right is in the preparation of the design. Once completed, I will seal the scrape or scratch with a fixer spray to set the makeup.

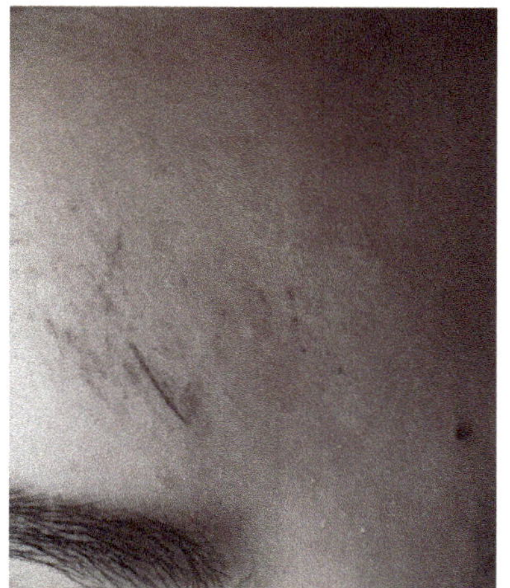

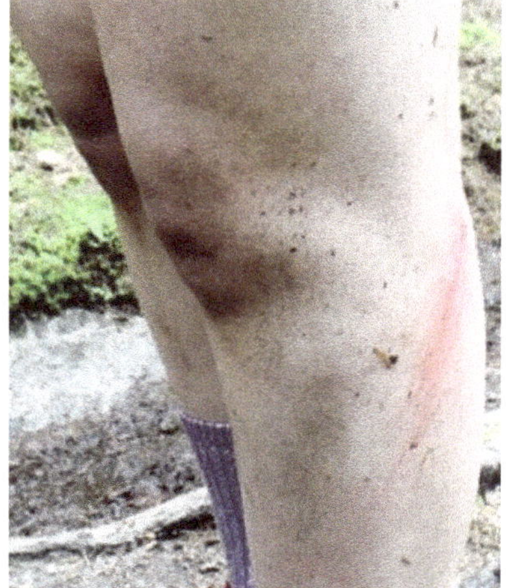

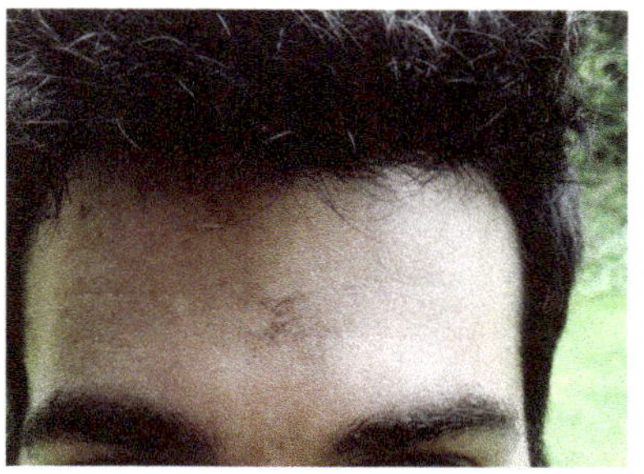

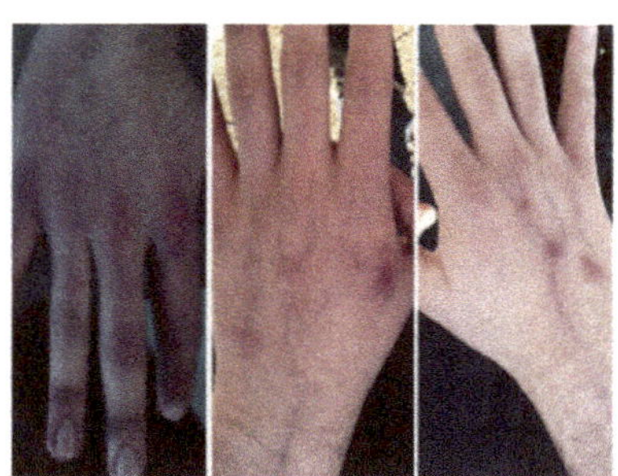

## SCARS

In January of 2017, I was part of the crew on an unforgettable independent film that was about the heroin epidemic taking place at the time. The filming locations were breathtaking, from the cranberry bog farm with a horse stable, to the coastline of the ocean, and finally to a mysterious house of heartbreak in the small town of Cape Cod, Massachusetts.

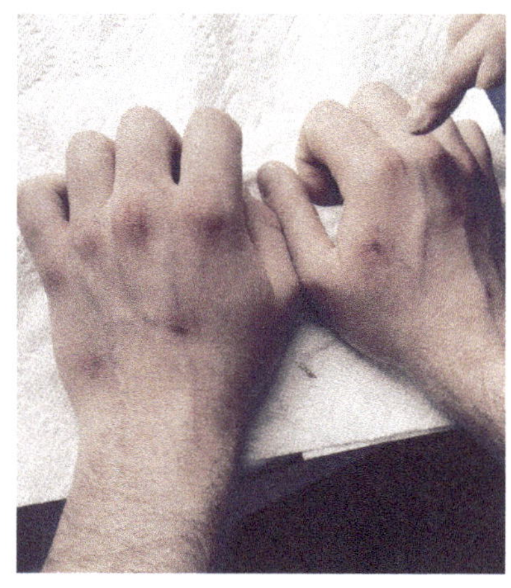

This movie touched so many of us. It felt as if we were filming this documentary in real time!

When I was told I would be doing SFX MU on the hands of the main character, I needed to know how old the scars were and if they were from open wounds or chronic healing wounds.

Documenting each step is vital for touchups as well as reshoots. I take photographs in color and black-and-white. Seeing it all come together is nothing short of surreal.

## SFX MUA First Aid Kit

As an SFX MUA, it's essential to be prepared for any situation that involves simulated injuries. To ensure smooth operation and creative consistency, I always carry a fully stocked SFX first aid kit with me to set.

The contents of my SFX first aid kit are carefully selected to cover a wide range of minor to more dramatic injury simulations. These items are practical for both quick fixes and to help maintain the realism of the injury. They also ensure continuity during filming.

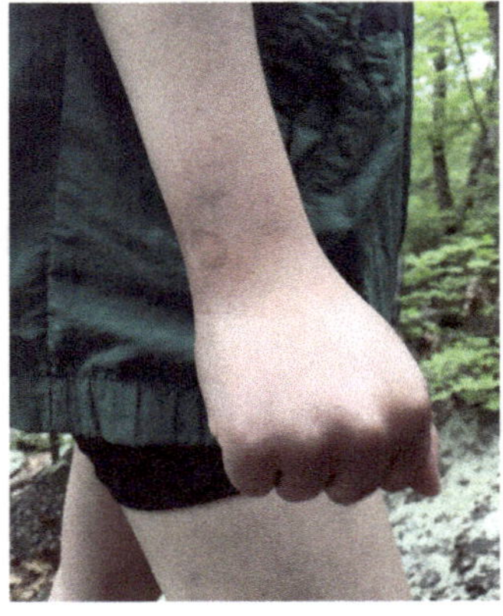

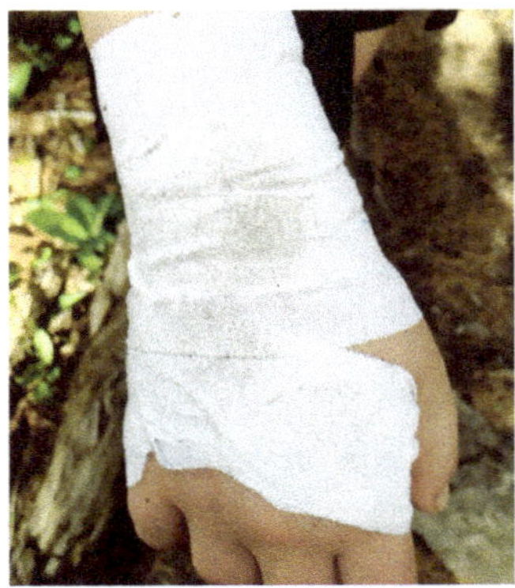

An injury was sustained by an actor who portrayed a character who fell and fractured their wrist. Having the actor's hand bandaged for the remaining week of filming shaved off sixty extra minutes in my makeup chair.

- ☐ **Bandages** (multiple sizes)
- ☐ **Pre-made stitches** (butterfly stitches)
- ☐ **White medical tape** (assorted widths)
- ☐ **Sterile gauze** (roll and square pads)
- ☐ **Splints** (assorted styles for limbs and joints)

## Liquid Tooth Discoloration

During prep, I start by placing small pieces of gauze under the actor's top and bottom lips to keep the area clean and allow the teeth to dry fully. I begin with a light stain, then check in with the executive producer to ensure we're achieving the desired effect, and finally, I'll adjust and build the look as needed based on their feedback.

**Important considerations when applying a liquid tooth product:**

- ☐ Prioritize safety whenever tooth discoloration is required by the script. Follow manufacturers' instructions carefully to ensure safety and effectiveness.
- ☐ Use only safe, professional-grade liquid tooth discoloration products.
- ☐ Always perform a patch test before application.
- ☐ Discuss and clarify during pre-production to understand the level of discoloration needed.
- ☐ Stock your kit with a range of shades from light stains to deep discoloration.
- ☐ Include a nicotine shade for smoker effects and black for missing tooth illusions.
- ☐ Apply color theory to mix custom shades tailored to the character's needs.
- ☐ Aim for a believable transformation that aligns with the manuscript's vision.

# Setting Powders and Setting Sprays

Setting powders and setting sprays are indispensable tools for creating flawless, long-lasting SFX MU looks. They ensure that your hard work is locked in place and can withstand the demands of both the environment and the production itself. Setting powders and sprays play a crucial role in keeping makeup in place, resisting smudging, and providing a smooth, matte finish.

Your collection might include, like mine, six base-tone setting powder colors, along with white and deep brown, allowing you to create an endless variety of shades.

To prepare my array of customized powders, I start by visiting the local dollar store to pick up small two-inch by two-inch plastic containers. I can usually purchase these in packs of ten. These containers are perfect for my "scientific work" of mixing and labeling formulas before packing my cases and heading to a film set. Don't forget to write the exact formula for each customized blend on the cover of each using a black fine-point permanent sharpie marker.

In extreme heat, especially during the summer months, I rely heavily on rice setting powder. Its incredible moisture-absorbing properties make it ideal for hot, humid environments, ensuring the makeup doesn't melt or break down. It really does work!

A setting spray can be incorporated upon the completion of applying camouflage makeup or a waterproof, aqua-based product. Setting spray acts as a sealant, locking the makeup in place and providing an added layer of protection.

# Makeup Carrying Cases

I have numerous SFX MU cases. My adhesives, blood products, and removers each have their own metal case, as they are liquids. All dry products will go into a separate case, as I never take the chance of packing liquid products and dry ingredients together in case a liquid bottle breaks or opens. I've been there and done that, not fun!

## Airbrushing Compressor and Liquid Gas (CO2)

When it comes to choosing between utilizing an airbrush compressor or a $CO_2$ system, know that they both propel air through a hose into the airbrush gun, where it mixes with liquid makeup to create a fine mist that is applied to the skin. Pressing the trigger will control airflow, drawing product from the reservoir for a precise application. Adjustable airflow and product flow provide exceptional control, allowing for both detailed designs and smooth, even coverage over larger areas of the body.

## Key Benefits of CO₂ Airbrush Systems

Using $CO_2$ enhances flexibility by offering makeup artists a versatile alternative to traditional compressors.

- ☐ Portable: Lightweight and easy to transport
- ☐ No Electricity Required: Perfect for remote or outdoor use
- ☐ Consistent Performance: Delivers steady, reliable airflow for even application

Using an airbrush compressor or $CO_2$ may seem daunting initially, but don't let that deter you. Enrolling in a specialized course can greatly enhance your skills, providing valuable insights into the handling and maintenance of your airbrush equipment. Working alongside an experienced professional can further unlock your creative potential, enabling you to express your artistry with confidence.

I would like to extend my appreciation for the input on $CO_2$ airbrushing to my favorite airbrush artist and dear friend, Ginny

Colangelo, also known as "The Boston Face Painter." Ginny is an accomplished specialist makeup artist and has worked on numerous films. I am grateful for her encouragement and support throughout my artistic journey.

## Tattoo Transfer Paper

It's easy to get your hands on tattoo transfer paper. My advice is to stay in close contact with the executive producer to confirm the desired look for this element. I remember reading a manuscript that described a twenty-eight-year-old man with an American flag tattoo on the outer side of his upper right arm. To prepare, I gathered a visual collection of several American flag tattoo designs to present at the first pre-production meeting. This allowed me to order the exact tattoo transfer the executive producer wanted. In fact, I ordered three flag tattoos, two to have as backups.

Usually, I'm a magician, and I make real tattoos disappear by applying camouflage makeup. Whether I'm hiding a tattoo or creating one, I always strive for authenticity. Adding tattoo transfer papers to my SFX MU kit was a decision I made at the beginning of my career to ensure I could craft a tattoo in a matter of minutes.

## Silicone and Latex Prosthetics

Silicone and latex prosthetics are essential materials for an advanced SFX MUA, which I do not have extensive training in. These are used to create realistic three-dimensional pieces like wounds, scars, creature features, and more.

Both prosthetic materials have unique properties that make them suitable for specific applications. Silicone prosthetics are valued for their durability, flexibility, and ability to mimic the texture and translucency of human skin, making them ideal for close-up shots and high-resolution filming. Latex prosthetics, on the other hand, are lightweight and cost-effective, often chosen for larger-scale applications or areas requiring extensive coverage.

Working with these materials requires in-depth training and a strong understanding of sculpting, molding, and casting techniques. Creating prosthetics involves several stages, including designing the piece, sculpting it to perfection, molding it using appropriate materials, and finally casting it in silicone or latex. Proper painting and blending techniques are also critical to seamlessly integrating the prosthetic with the actor's skin. This level of detail and craftsmanship ensures the prosthetics deliver a lifelike appearance, enhancing the overall effect for film, theater, or live events.

## SFX MU PUTTY

I use putty to create realistic textures all over the skin, such as raised scars, wounds, or other deformities. It's a versatile product that I can mold and shape directly onto the actor's clean skin. Once I sculpt the putty to the desired effect, I'll blend it into the surrounding skin before applying any additional makeup or coloring. Always follow the manufacturer's instructions, as each has its own way of applying its product.

## SFX MOLDING WAX

Molding Wax is impressive for creating more defined features, such as a deep cut or reshaping an actor's nose or chin. Before I begin the application, I will slightly warm the molding wax with the palms of my hands to make it more pliable, then sculpt it into the needed shape. After it's applied, I'll smooth it out to blend, then add a sealant to ensure it stays in place.

Both SFX MU putty and molding wax allow me to create unbelievable SFX MU looks that hold up to the demands of a full day of filming.

## Makeup Dirt Bag

My makeup dirt bag is one of my favorite tools for adding realistic dirt effects to an actor's skin or hair. It's a small fabric bag filled with fine ground powders, often a mix of crushed fuller's earth, cocoa powder, charcoal, or other natural-looking materials. The fabric is porous enough to allow the powder to escape in a controlled way when the bag is patted or squeezed. Never bring a MUA dirt bag into a live filming set, as dust will get everywhere. Any actor touch-ups will be done in a separate area.

When using a makeup dirt bag, go for authenticity. Start by consulting the manuscript and your pre-production notes to determine how dirty or weathered the character needs to look. For example, are they a miner, a soldier on the battlefield, or just someone who had a rough fall in the middle of the woods?

For applying, I gently pat or shake the makeup dirt bag over the areas I want dirty on the skin. I focus on exposed areas like the face, arms, or hands, where dirt would naturally accumulate. I make sure to press the bag lightly into the skin to ensure the "dirt" doesn't just sit on the surface. Sometimes I use my hands to blend or rub the powder in for a more smudged or embedded look. If the scene involves sweat or water, I might mist the area lightly before applying the powder, so it clings better and appears even grittier. It's all about layering until it looks just right. The key is to always start light, then add more if needed, but it's harder to take away without redoing everything. Cleanup is simple, since most powders can be brushed off easily or removed with a damp cloth.

## BLACK EYE BRUISE

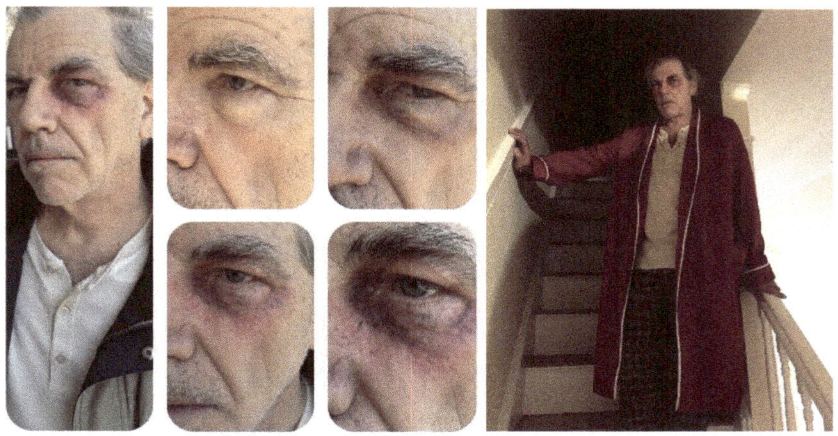

Actor Ralph Cushen receives a good shiner in Director Jonathan Heutmaker's film *Stella*.

I remember when I was hired as the director of HMU for the independent film *Stella*. The scene we were shooting took place just eight hours after the main character had been in a barroom brawl. This meant the character's black eye needed to look fresh, raw, and swollen.

As always, I practice what I preach and proceeded to do my research. I pulled out my trusted special effects morgue reference book, which includes a detailed photographic progression of black eyes, documenting the changes from the moment of injury through the first three days of healing.

During our pre-production meeting, the executive producer initially saw Ralph's eye as black and blue with a touch of yellow. I explained that the presence of yellow typically indicates an older injury that's already in the healing stages, not something that would appear just eight hours after impact. According to the script, Ralph's injury was supposed to be much fresher, swollen, discolored, and visibly tender. That meant we needed to reflect on the early trauma, not the later stages of bruising.

Once I showed the producer the reference images and broke down the stages of bruising, he understood and agreed with my more realistic approach. This is exactly why thorough research and open communication are essential, especially when SFX MU effects are involved. You always want the final look to feel authentic to the manuscript. This time, the mission was accomplished!

## CAMOUFLAGE CREAM MAKEUP

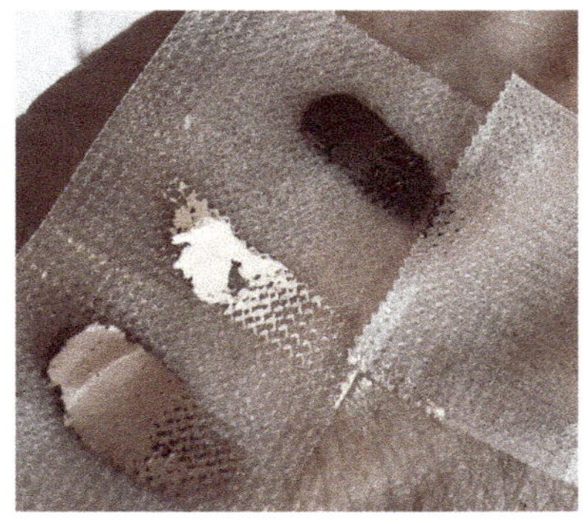

Clear medical tape on top of my hand that I used to warm up camouflage makeup.

I've spent the last forty years of my career mastering the art of using camouflage cream makeup to conceal all kinds of imperfections, such as scars, age spots, bruises, vitiligo, and burn marks. I quickly realized that I could make these imperfections temporarily disappear and also re-create them. This is where I use the one-to-ten color method that I discussed previously in Chapter 3. With this method, I've been able to develop hundreds of custom colors and tones, giving me the flexibility to achieve just the right effect for any situation and lighting.

When I need maximum skin coverage, I reach for my camouflage cream palette. It has a thick, stiff texture at first, but softens with body heat. To make it easier to work with, I apply a few layers of clear medical tape to the top of my hand. This gives the product a surface to warm up and melt into a creamier consistency, making application much smoother. I consider this a miracle product with its ability to conceal tattoos, birthmarks, and discolorations. It's a total lifesaver!

I once worked on an infomercial shoot where I had to completely rethink my makeup approach when I saw the main actor enter my room. Her face was flushed and covered in hives with swollen blotches.

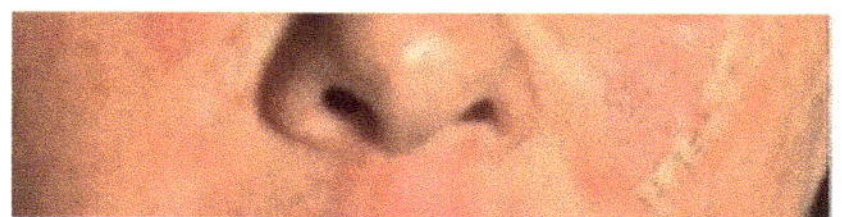 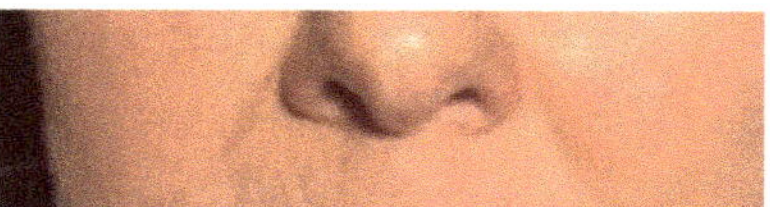

I once worked on an infomercial shoot where I had to completely rethink my makeup approach when I saw the main actor enter my room (see picture above).

Her hands were visibly shaking, and my heart was racing.

Thankfully, there was a doctor on set. I approached him and suggested it might be contact dermatitis from the hotel, though I made it clear I wasn't diagnosing. He confirmed my suspicion and suspected the hotel linens were the cause. With no open sores or blisters, he gave me the go-ahead to proceed.

I was nervous about how the actor's skin would react to the camouflage cream makeup. The crew was convinced the day was a loss, but I focused on calming her down and carefully concealing the redness and texture.

Before the lighting test, I filled in the cinematographer and gaffer about the swelling so they could adjust accordingly. The cinematographer widened the shot to avoid drawing attention to the actor's face. In the end, the infomercial was a success, and the camouflage makeup held up beautifully under the hot lights. That day reminded me how vital it is to stay calm, adapt quickly, and always have the right tools on hand.

## Tattoo Coverage with Camouflage Makeup

When I am planning to cover a tattoo and the area has been previously injured, I occasionally encounter some resistance from the skin. It's common to see a raised hive or welt start to form on the surface of the skin. This is simply the skin's way of reacting to past trauma. Knowing this, I always take extra care with these applications, understanding that the skin might "fight back" due to its heightened sensitivity. For this reason, I keep a cold cloth nearby. If I notice the skin is reacting, I will gently press the cold cloth to the area. This helps to smooth the skin and reduce any swelling or redness, which is especially important when working on sensitive areas that need coverage. By calming down the skin before setting the makeup, I ensure a smoother, more effective application that holds up well under the demands of hot lights.

When I finish the application, I use a waterproof fixer spray to set the makeup. Once the fixer spray dries completely, it will ensure the makeup becomes water-resistant, muscle-resistant, heat-resistant, and has lasting coverage. When it comes time to remove camouflage makeup, use an oil-based cleansing lotion to get the job done.

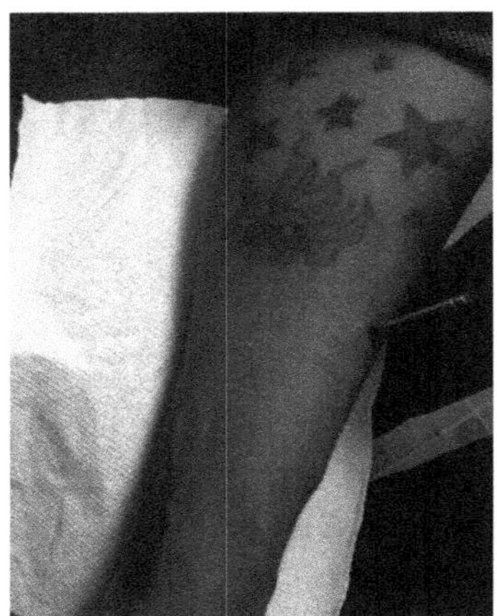

Before and after pictures of a camouflage makeup application to the arm of an actor, whose character did not have tattoos.

## SFX MU for Aging

Knowing the age of the character and the age of the actor is just the beginning. I also need to know the socioeconomic environment the character grew up in. Was he poor, middle class, or rich? Did he work indoors or outdoors in different weather conditions? This helps me capture the unique signs of aging that match the character's life experiences.

When I'm adding facial hair to an actor, I tell the actor not to shave, as this is a sure way to help me age him for the character.

# Latex Wrinkling

When aging an actor, there are several techniques you can use to create a believable transformation. One foundational method involves the use of latex and a stipple sponge to simulate fine wrinkles.

First, identify key wrinkle zones. Typically, you'll focus on the forehead, the corners of the eyes, and around the mouth.

- ☐ Apply latex using a stipple sponge by stretching the skin lightly in the area you're working on, then stipple a thin layer of latex using an on-off dabbing motion.

- ☐ Allow it to partially dry until the latex becomes tacky but not fully set.

- ☐ Release the skin, and as the latex relaxes, it creates fine wrinkling that mimics aged skin.

- ☐ Once the latex is dry, build depth and realism using a combination of cream-based colors and powders. Focus on shading and highlighting the natural contours of the face to emphasize the aged texture.

- ☐ Don't forget the hands and neck areas that can break the illusion if left untouched. These details help make the aging effect more believable from all angles.

- ☐ Finally, set your work with either a setting powder or a fixer spray to ensure it holds up under hot lights.

# Alternative to Latex

If the actor has a latex allergy or you're working under time constraints, you can still achieve an effective aged look without prosthetics:

- ☐ Hand-draw fine lines with a makeup pencil or brush, following natural expression lines.

- ☐ Use cream-based contour and highlight products to create the illusion of sagging skin, hollowed cheeks, and eye bags.
- ☐ Apply color correction or layering techniques to create the uneven pigmentation often seen in aged skin.

Always study reference images of aged faces across different ethnicities and age groups. Not all aging looks the same, and attention to subtle differences can make your work stand out. Practice both latex and non-latex methods so you can adapt to different actors, roles, and production needs.

A few years ago, I was hired as an HMU to age a male actor for a television commercial for a bank in Maine. For this specific look, I had to pre-plan by asking the actor to grow out his hair, sideburns, mustache, and beard for the next five weeks until I saw him on set. I was to transform this actor into a character that was to be aged three different times during the filming.

What did I do for the first look? I added a temporary deep brown hair rinse to the actor's natural gray and brown hair color to make him look younger. Then I did the same for his beard, mustache, and sideburns. When it came to doing the fifty-year-old look, I took out the dark brown hair rinse and hand-painted grayer streaks to his already existing gray and brown hair. Same for his facial hair. For the sixty-five-year-old look, I made his hair look seventy-five percent gray and twenty-five percent white. The beard, mustache, and sideburns became whiter with a slight gray streak throughout them.

## Creating with Crepe Hair

In my line of work, mastering crepe hair application has become an essential skill. I rely on crepe hair for its technical precision and creative flexibility. It allows me to fully bring to life the character envisioned by the executive producer.

Working with crepe hair is one of the most rewarding techniques in designing and executing SFX MU transformations. This highly versatile material, made from tightly woven wool and typically sold in braided form, is indispensable for creating realistic facial and body hair effects, including beards, mustaches, sideburns, chest hair, and even eyebrows.

As you advance in your career as an SFX MUA, you'll likely use crepe hair across a wide range of projects to reshape and redefine the character that an actor will portray.

At the pre-production meeting, I'll ask key questions: Is the character from a working-class background and likely to have a rough beard or unkempt mustache? Or are they middle-class, with a more maintained appearance? Perhaps they're part of the elite, sporting a carefully groomed style that reflects the fashion of the time. These subtle distinctions are essential for creating an authentic, historically accurate look that enhances the character's life on screen.

## Preparing Crepe Hair

One of the most important things to consider when designing a look utilizing crepe hair is how crucial it is to accurately match the actor's natural hair color or use a wig already made.

Crepe hair needs to be prepared properly, or you'll end up throwing the hair and your money away. I cut only the desired length from the braid that I will need for the design, then spend time unwinding the hair by separating the fibers with my hands to the degree of thickness needed. Once unwinded, I will follow the pre-production approval designs and style the crepe hair. If needed, I will utilize flat irons and curling irons. This step is time-consuming, so be patient. Taking training on how to work with crepe hair from a professional is well worth it!

## TRANSPORTING CREPE HAIR

All crepe hair designs are pre-made and brought to the set in metal cases. Once on set, I meticulously apply each hairpiece to the actor according to the design, ensuring precise placement.

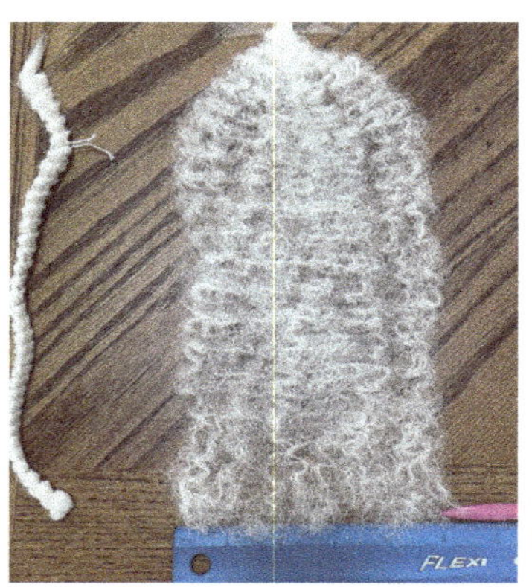

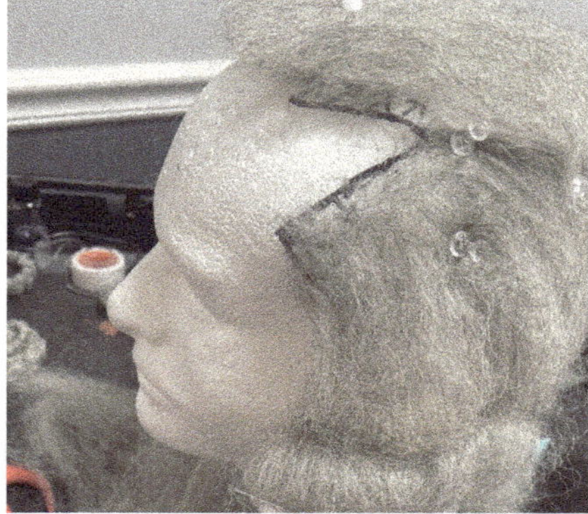

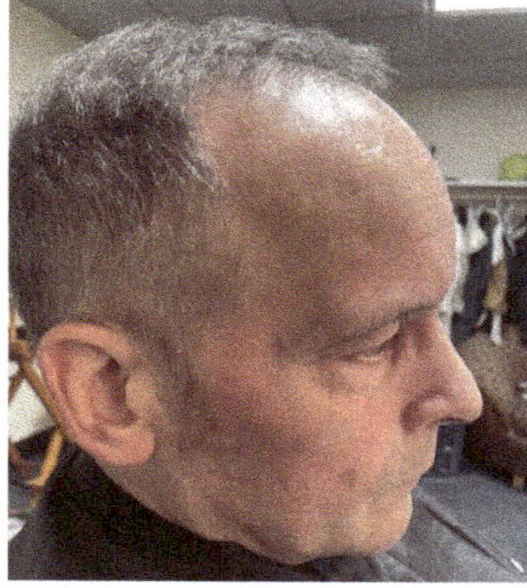 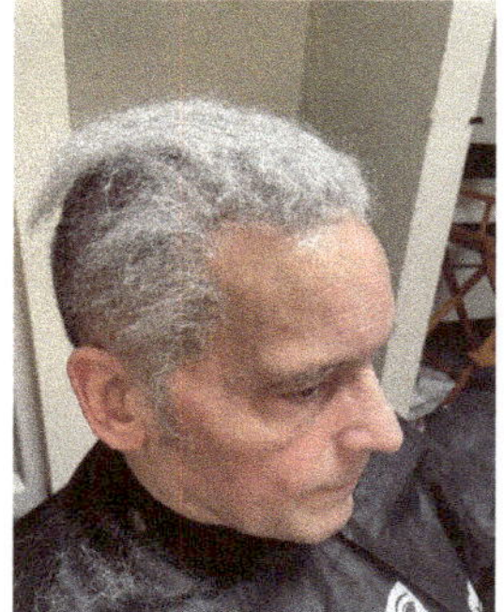 

I custom-made the above hairpiece for actor Jay Thomas Fox for a documentary about the American Revolutionary War. I placed each individual piece of crepe hair onto a wig head.

Actor Jack Shea wears crepe hair, portraying two different characters for the documentary *Half the History*.

 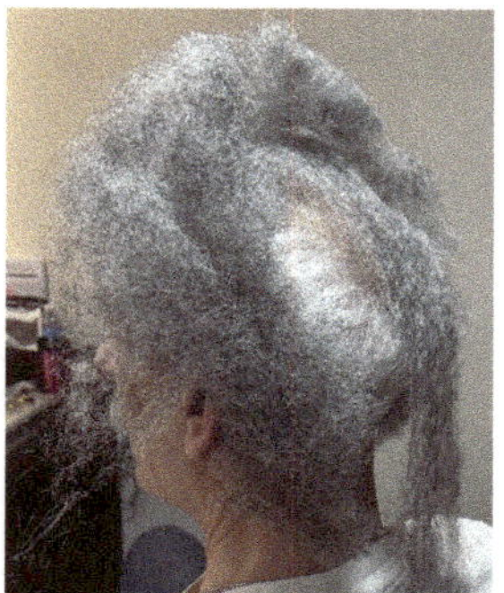 

Actor Michael Dellorto was transformed in under three hours for *Fly Me to the Moon*.

In the summer and early fall of 2023, I traveled to five different states as part of an awesome film crew from Northern Lights Productions to work on a Frederick Douglass documentary. Of all the documentary films I have worked on, this one left a lasting impression on me. I was so ignorant of who this hero was, and I'm angry that I was never educated about him in school. It was an honor to be part of this team!

Actor James Milord portrays Frederick Douglass in his early years.
James's transformation took two and a half hours.

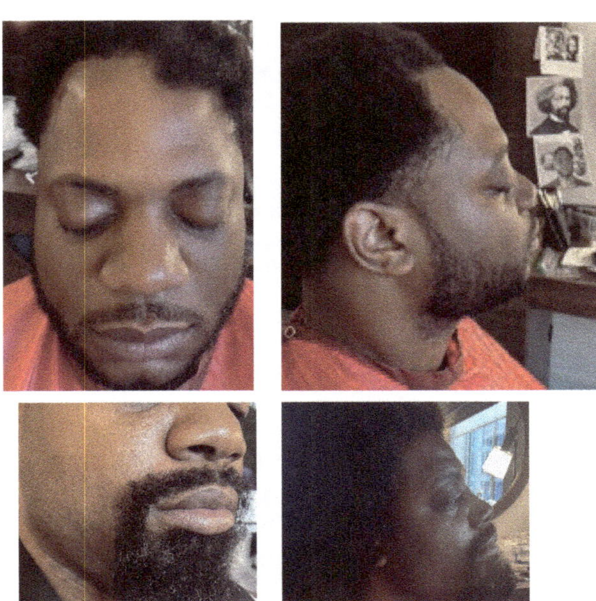

# Mustaches, Beards, and Sideburns

Mustaches, beards, and sideburns might seem like a minor detail to some, but to me, it's an art form that breathes life into a character. In the film world, those small touches hold the power to transform an actor and make a character truly authentic. I pour my heart into every detail, ensuring my work not only meets expectations but becomes a reliable part of the storytelling magic.

The special effects adhesives and spirit gums to adhere crepe hair come in many forms, and I suggest you thoroughly research the various kinds and their specific uses. For example, I personally avoid using water-soluble spirit gum on areas like a man's top lip, sideburns, or eyebrows because it doesn't hold up well on sweaty skin. I learned this the hard way when I had to reapply an actor's sideburns many times due to his sweating.

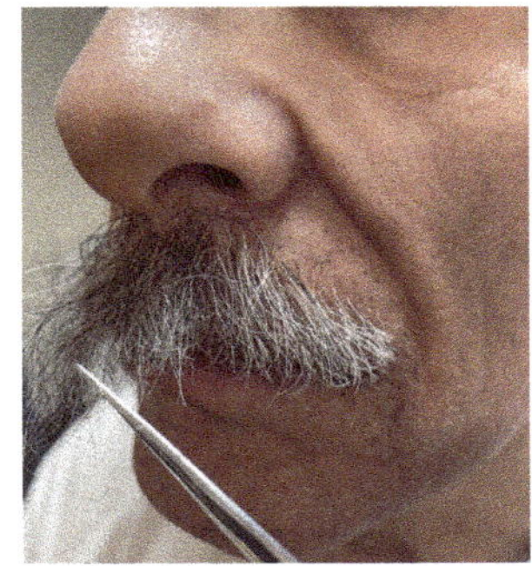

Actor Michael Dellorto sat patiently while I trimmed off the excess crepe hair I applied over his grown-out stubble.

**Here is my step-by-step guide I use to apply crepe hair:**
- ☐ **Prep the Skin**

Clean the actor's face with a gentle cleanser and toner to remove oils and dirt. Skip moisturizer to ensure maximum adhesive grip.

- ☐ **Apply Adhesive:**

Choose the right adhesive based on the location to be applied on the body and wear time.

- ☐ **First layer:** Apply a thin layer to prepped skin and let it fully dry to prevent lifting from sweat.
- ☐ **Second layer:** Add spirit gum, wait until tacky, then press crepe hair into place. Secure edges well and blend with makeup for a natural look.

### 3. Layer the Crepe Hair

Build gradually, trimming and shaping as you go. Work in small sections for control over density and direction.

- ☐ **Mustaches/Beards:** Follow natural growth pattern, using a rat-tail comb to guide.
- ☐ **Sideburns:** Apply along the hairline and blend into existing hair.
- ☐ **Chest Hair:** Use larger sections, following natural growth.
- ☐ **Eyebrows:** Use fine sections, matching brow shape, then trim for realism.

### 4. On-Set Maintenance

- ☐ Keep an actor's kit with you for quick touch-ups. Include adhesive, comb, and small tools.

### 5. Removal Tips

- ☐ Remove gently to avoid skin irritation or damage.
- ☐ Use removers formulated for your application products.
- ☐ Cleanse skin afterward and rehydrate.

## Wigs and Hairpieces

Discussing wigs and hairpieces can be challenging during the first phase of pre-production. Your first question should be: *"Does the production have the budget to purchase wigs, hairpieces, and crepe hair if the script calls for them?"*

Your next question should be: *"Who will be in charge of purchasing them?"*

Many times, you may be handed a box of wigs and asked if you can work with them. Sometimes you can, but most of the time they turn out to be cheap ones used at Halloween. Yuck!

If there's no budget for wigs, then you'll need to work with the actor's natural hair and, if necessary, suggest to the costume director that a hat or period-appropriate head covering might be used to address issues such as short hair.

Whenever you're dealing with wigs and hairpieces, it's vital to collaborate with the costume director, as this is the person who truly speaks your language when it comes to achieving the complete look. For example, a 1750s hairstyle on a forty-year-old high-society Southern woman attending a wedding has specific details you'll need to capture. The more information you gather, the more precise and authentic your HMU designs will be.

I recommend that you do not purchase any wigs or hairpieces, especially with your own money, until you've confirmed with the executive producer and the costume designer in pre-production to make sure these items are within the budget. If I make a purchase with the executive producer's permission, they'll reimburse me, or I'll use their money to purchase it.

Above, actor Andrea Lyman portrayed a young and an elderly woman as the title character in a documentary about Ellen Garrison's life. Andrea wore the same wig for both characters. To age the wig, I added streaks of white and gray hair paint with a synthetic brush. The process took approximately forty-five minutes.

It's a smart business practice to keep all your expense receipts for materials in a safe place and submit them to the appropriate person for reimbursement. Always keep a copy of the receipts you submit for your own records. In most cases, you'll receive two separate checks from the production company: one for your subcontracted services and another for the supplies you've submitted as reimbursable expenses.

## 6  FINAL KEY THOUGHTS

☐ Define your career path within the SFX MUA market.

☐ Learn basic SFX MU for entry-level opportunities.

☐ Understand what is needed to build a basic SFX MU kit.

☐ Design SFX MU looks that align with the manuscript and the character's needs.

☐ Gain knowledge in designing and creating crepe hair for realistic effects.

☐ Collaborate closely with the costume designer to ensure cohesive designs.

Actor Jay Thomas Fox on set with Steve Sherrick, director of photography.

# Chapter 7

Now you know the steps that took me from dreaming about being on a film set as an MUA to living it! I started by developing my skills and then pursuing film-specific jobs so I could eventually step onto any set with confidence. I built a portfolio that spoke for me before I introduced myself, that showed my range of artistry and the power to transform a face into a story. I gained real-world experience by saying yes to student films, independent film projects, and assisting opportunities that honed my skills and expanded my network. Finally, I learned about the film industry inside and out, its etiquette, its pace, and the importance of constant growth.

## Recap

- ☐ Develop your skills: specialize in film makeup
- ☐ Build your portfolio: show your range, quality, and artistry
- ☐ Gain experience: join student films, indie projects, and assist
- ☐ Network in the film world: join, attend, and connect
- ☐ Understand the film industry: master etiquette, time, and trends

Whether you're just starting out or dreaming of one day being the director of the makeup department for a film, you now have the roadmap. I hope this book gives you confidence, clarity, and inspiration to take the first step and keep moving forward until the credits roll on your own success story.

Thank you for letting me part of your journey!

Rhonda

# Check Out Your Research Skills!

<u>Exercise #1</u>

Choose an MUA who has won an award for *Best MUA for a Motion Film*. How did this artist's work impact the outcome of the film through makeup? (refer to chapter 1)

<u>Exercise #2</u>

Take an inventory of your current makeup kit, tools, and equipment. Make a list of what you need to add to your kit. (refer to chapter 2)

<u>Exercise #3</u>

Compile pictures virtually to compose a "portfolio morgue" for the year 1850. Research the fashions for women, men, teenagers, and children. Include 1850s hairstyles, makeup looks, plus clothing styles. Include 1850s facial hair designs for young males, middle-aged men, and seniors. (refer to chapters 2 and 3)

<u>Exercise #4</u>

Research templates and examples of film call sheets on the internet. Spend time getting familiarized with the many different types of call sheets. (refer to chapter 4)

# Acknowledgements

My journey would not have been possible without the love, patience, and belief in me from my husband, Allen. I am also deeply grateful for the support and encouragement I received from my family, friends, and colleagues throughout the process of writing this book. Each of you has played a meaningful role in my life and I extend my heartfelt thanks to each of you.

A very special thank you to Joyce Poirier, my living angel for over forty years. Your inspiration, your patience through countless rewrites, your thoughtful corrections, and your steady guidance have all been gifts I will never forget. Your encouragement lifted me in the moments when life felt overwhelming, reminding me to keep going and believe in this story. I am endlessly grateful to you. And now, after all the hard work, we can finally celebrate this book in print.

A special acknowledgement to the first group of people to witness my journey unfold in writing. Thank you all for taking the time to be involved as a beta reader. Your input was valuable to the success of my book. Thank you from the bottom of my heart Allie Humenuk, An Hinds, Andrea Lyman, Anne Tubiolo, Ashley St. George, Christine King, Christine St. George, Cinthia Chen, Danielle Bryant, Dawn Sinibaldi, Deb Pearson, Denise Mahoney, Diane Piper, Diane Sheehan, Dida Hagan, Doreen Cusolito, Jaclyn Luongo, Jessica Mogauro, Julie Sinatra, Kristin Cummings, Linda Girard, Madonna Harris, Michelle D'Allaird-Brenner, Paula Currier, Rozy Dahlstedt, Ruthann Armstrong, Shirley Sarpi, Terry Kenney, Toni Elliot, and Ursula Burton.

Thank you to Steve Harrison and his devoted group of bestselling authors and trainers at Bradley Communications for making this possible! A special shoutout to my incredible talented writing coach Shannon Hazel, my awesome editor Valerie Costa, and the talented Christy Day who designed my book and Gina Keiser my proofreader.

# About the Author

**RHONDA CUMMINGS** pulls back the curtain *on Behind the Scenes as a Makeup Artist for Film,* offering readers an unfiltered look into her decades-long journey through the beauty and film industries. With over forty years as a makeup artist, cosmetologist, aesthetician, and licensed instructor, she delivers hard-earned insights for those serious about breaking into film makeup.

Starting her career at age eighteen, Rhonda achieved her dream of becoming department head for hair and makeup for film at age fifty-two. Now sixty-seven, she has led the hair and makeup departments for more than a dozen independent films, documentaries, and television projects, while training over 1,000 aspiring makeup artists. Her story blends memoir with practical guidance that covers everything she's experienced from pre-production demands to on-set pressures, collaboration, and ethics, making this book both inspiring and instructional.

A former salon owner, advanced school owner, educator, and skin care distributor, today she freelances as hair and makeup department head for two Massachusetts-based production companies specializing in historical documentaries, museum quality filming, and commercial film projects. Her expertise in makeup, hair, and wig styling has made her a sought-after leader on set.

Rhonda's career is a testament to the value of comprehensive training, adaptability, and creative problem-solving under pressure. For inquiries about training or speaking engagements she can be reached at rhonda@ rcmakeupartist.com.

# Sign up to stay in touch!

You'll receive Rhonda's newsletter with upcoming events, book signing dates, podcasts, expert tips, and behind-the-scenes stories from on-set!